SWANA DYKES

SWANA DYKES

EDITED BY KHADIJA PITTS-CEESAY
AND NIKKI LUNA

Sinister Wisdom

Sinister Wisdom 142
Fall 2026

Editor and Publisher: Julie Enszer
Cover and interior designed by Nieves Guerra.

Cover image by Micaela Kaibni Raen
Front: *Tetas' Tears (Queer Tatreez)*
Back: *Zahri Moon with Feathers (Queer Tatreez)*
Media: Multi-media (digitally stitched Tatreez, acrylic painting, and photography).
Made in the style of Queer Tatreez. Used with Permission. See artist statement in book.

Previous Publication Credits:

Sarah E. Azizi: "Make A Wish" and "Jealousy" were previously published in Sarah's debut poetry collection, *Make A Wish,* in 2025 by ELJ Editions.

Christina Hajjar: "Diaspora Daughter / Diaspora Dyke" was previously published in Christina's self-published *Diaspora Daughter / Diaspora Dyke* zine in 2020 and *Bahr Magazine – Issue 2* in 2021.

Amal Ishaque: "Iftah Ya Simsim" was previously published by *The Ex-Puritan Magazine* (then known as *The Puritan Magazine*) in 2019.
Diya Abbas: "I-11 Islamabad" was previously published by *Lakeer Magazine* in 2025.

Sinister Wisdom, Inc.
2333 McIntosh Road - Dover, FL 33527
sinisterwisdom@gmail.com - www.sinisterwisdom.org
First edition, October 2026
ISBN: 978-1-970841-00-8 print
ISBN: 978-1-970841-01-5 ebook
Library of Congress Call Number: 2026009401
Printed in the U.S.

CONTENTS

NOTES FOR A SPECIAL ISSUE

Ghazal

The air smells metallic, humid with blood seeping into the river,
sirens call to each other like banshees searching for home.

Discarded hand, lost foot, forgotten limb after limb covering the ground.
The sky is too beige to look up, decorated in phosphorus yet I call this home.

The ground rumbles and comes loose beneath my kitchen floor
While mother clings to her pots and pans that made voyage from her home.

Our mouths spill sewage, curses and fear into the air, asking when our time has come.
We listen to marching feet like death drums that ring across the alley behind my home.

We, who are forced to make room for others, we
who are ignored for giving up our lives, our hope, our homes.

I watch while the world watches back, blank and doe-eyed at our fear,
watch them give our killers money, permission to invade our home.

I scream through the lungs of another child without a mother, search the rubble
for a hint of my family, try to piece together my home

with unstable fingers. Our blood is forever embedded in the cracked walls of every
mosque, waiting until Allah calls us home.

—Khadija Pitts-Ceesay

SWANA, which is an acronym for South West Asia and North Africa, is a geographical term utilized instead of the Western term "the Middle East." Categorization of such a vast region is complicated, as the varying positionalities of people who reside in and are diasporic to the region are affected by ancestry, nationalism, globalization, and histories of colonization. In creating *SWANA Dykes*, we wanted to showcase the variety of mediums and themes that SWANA artists are utilizing in their works. We're proud to highlight artists who are engaged in their communities through their artistry and activism—artists who are fighting for a world stewarded by Indigenous Peoples.

We are immensely grateful to our contributors for their generosity in sharing their perspective and heart through their artistry. Thank you, KT Abadir-Mullally, Diya Abbas, Andrea Abi-Karam, Noor Al-Dayeh, Sarah E. Azizi, Elias Bouderdaben, Mahru Elahi, Lamya H, Christina Hajjar, Amal Ishaque, Nour Kamel, Juanita Kirton, Najlaa Manout, Melina McConatha, Miqlae, Janine Mogannam, Anna Rose Naim, Amir Patros, Arielle Zaytoun Sonnenschein, Hanan Tuffaha, Micaela Kaibni Raen, Eva Roslin, and WIDAD for your essential offerings to this collection.

These artists explore many urgent topics: the sacredness of transgender people and gender non-conformity, resistance against militarism, policing, and genocide, the exploitative Kafala system, and archives as a tool of liberation. They make connections between different oppressive systems that seek to isolate marginalized peoples, illustrating how the recognition of interconnectedness is a necessary part of movement work. Artists additionally detail their personal experiences of sex, familial bonds, fashion, artistry, and relationships. While many of us have been coerced into xenophobic compartmentalization, these artists push back against legibility, depoliticization, and essentialism. Through making the crucial connections between the personal and political, the artists of *SWANA Dykes* contribute to the ever-evolving movement of artists envisioning a world beyond militarized borders.

It is essential that people who are living through the precarity of genocide, apartheid, occupation, war, and oppressive governments are centered in movement work. Anthologies alone cannot do the work of transforming our world. Please see our resource list at the end of the book, which includes a list of organizations doing mutual aid, fundraising, education, and solidarity work to support beloved people within and beyond the SWANA region. We want to acknowledge that *SWANA Dykes* is not a comprehensive representation of the religious, racial, cultural, sexual, or gender diversity of the SWANA region.

We dedicate this issue to our chosen family, to our relatives, to our kin stolen from us, to archives destroyed and forgotten, to those who never wanted to be documented, to Etel Adnan, to Sarah Hegazi, to our ancestors who line our path with synchronistic reminders, to our lovers, and to all who fight diligently for our collective future.

We hold to this truth: we are connected through water, through love, and through memory.

Khadija Pitts-Ceesay and Nikki Luna

October 2026

TEXTS

Khadija Pitts-Ceesay and Nikki Luna

< 104 **khadija** 🖤 >

Hey! Have you heard Pluto by Raveena? It reminded me of our conversation the other day!

yes I love that song!! 🫀 🥲 I'm down to exchange playlists!

Ooooh great idea! I'm down, I love new music! 😌

😘😘😘

Jennifer's Body
Nxdia

Choose Your Fighter
Nova Twins

In Your Dreams
Choked Up

miss construed
Nemahsis

Free 🅴
Little Simz

Still Thinkin' Bout Me
Amira Jazeera

These songs look sick! So excited!!

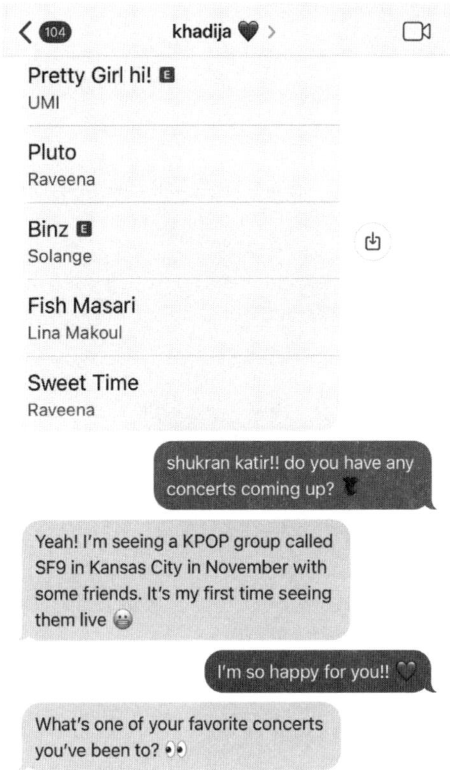

104
khadija 🖤
Pretty Girl hi! E
UMI
Pluto
Raveena
Binz E
Solange
Fish Masari
Lina Makoul
Sweet Time
Raveena
shukran katir!! do you have any concerts coming up?
Yeah! I'm seeing a KPOP group called SF9 in Kansas City in November with some friends. It's my first time seeing them live 😬
I'm so happy for you!! 🖤
What's one of your favorite concerts you've been to? 👀

104
khadija 🖤
I saw Little Simz in Chicago in 2019! She's such a talented lyricist and musician it meant a lot to me to see her live!
I've heard a couple Little Simz songs, that's so cool!!
Thanks for the playlist btw, I love exchanging music
See you at the next SWANA Dykes meeting 💋
see you soon habibti!

INTERVIEWS WITH LAMYA H

Khadija Pitts-Ceesay

KHADIJA: Hello!

LAMYA: Hi!

KHADIJA: How are you?

LAMYA: Good! How are you?

KHADIJA: I'm good! I just want to say before we start, I read your book almost a year ago and I don't think it's an exaggeration to say it literally changed my life. Everything that I felt about my religious or sexual identity was finally put into words. So, I just want to say thank you for putting out this book that I'm sure has healed a lot of people including myself.

LAMYA: That's incredible! Thank you so much for saying that, that's so, so sweet. When I wrote this book, I really hoped it would reach people that were queer and Muslim and it's wonderful to see the ways in which it does that, you know? It's been really cool and lovely.

KHADIJA: Yeah, I'm sure! So, what was the catalyst for writing the book? Did you have an experience that led up to it, or did you have something that kind of told you that you had to write this book? What was the idea behind it?

LAMYA: Honestly, it kind of just happened. I wish there was a better origin story to this book, but I kind of just lucked into it. I didn't set out to write this book. In fact, the person who is my agent now who I met way before I was even thinking about writing a book, she had always been like "Hey, when are you writing this book? You're gonna write a book!" and I was always like "what are you talking about?" I didn't grow up as a writer, I didn't take writing classes in college or high school. I just kind of fell into it because I would write these essays back in the time that people were publishing essays on the internet—you know that glorious period of time when people were putting a lot of personal writing out on the internet. And so, I wrote essays. Then all of a sudden, I found myself writing one of the chapters of the book as an essay, and it's actually one of the chapters nearest the end, the chapter on Hajr. I wrote that essay because I was thinking a lot about the situation I was in where me and my partner were going to visit my family and we were pretending to be friends. It was Eid so I was thinking a lot about Hajr and her sacrifice and the sacrifices me and my partner were making to be able to be around family. So, that chapter emerged from that, thinking about the silence of sacrifice. The sacrifices that are very visible versus the ones that aren't. Thinking about the sacrifice of Hajr versus the sacrifice of Ibrahim which in that story is seen as Ibrahim's—but I was thinking specifically about Hajr.

LAMYA: And when I wrote that chapter, I was like, "Wait, there are so many of these other chapters inside of me, where in some ways my whole life I've been thinking about this." I've been thinking about the ways in which the prophets and these other figures from the Quran were actually very human figures. There were people who made mistakes, and who made some questionable decisions, and were in difficult situations. And I'd always been thinking about those stories and stories from my life, and I found that I could write so many more of these chapters because in some ways I had been thinking about these stories my entire life.

LAMYA: From there the series of chapters kind of turned into a book and I was really lucky to work with an editor who was really good at taking these disparate chapters or essays and weaving them into a larger story. She made me think a lot about narrative arcs and how I want to arrange these chapters, what I'm trying to say, what are the bigger themes. So, the book kind of just happened. I feel like I lucked into it... That's my long rambling answer!

KHADIJA: That's really interesting, because when I was reading the chapters I recognized a lot of these stories, but I haven't read all of them and so it put it into a different perspective. It made sense. It made a lot more sense than what I was raised on. And so I'm really grateful for that because I was like, "Oh, I have to go back, read these stories, and look at them in a different way that is more helpful."

LAMYA: Yeah! I know you had your next question about what I'm hoping people get out of this book. One of the things that I want people to get out of this book is this ability to look at these stories that we've been told for so long and think of them through a really, really personal lens and to think of the Quran as this living, breathing text that we get to interpret too. I think so often, there's this way in which Islam is taught to us and in ways that can be really rigid and not expansive. Especially as queer Muslims, I think it's important to think of the text as living, breathing, and addressed to us.

KHADIJA: Right! I was reading and I was like, "Hmmm, sometimes these stories seem closer to me than I was taught." They make a lot more sense now. So yeah, I totally get that. While you were writing it, was there anything that you learned about yourself? Was there anything during the writing process that you thought, "Oh, I have to change this up?" Or maybe you learned something new about yourself or something unexpected?

LAMYA: I think the thing that I was not expecting, which in retrospect seems really silly, is the way in which writing would be healing. I feel like so often the things that I was writing about were things that had stuck with me and that were sitting inside me. I had to almost go back and revisit those memories and look back at them as an older person with more experience in the world and just have empathy for myself. I feel like it's often so easy to be really hard on yourself, especially at that moment. I found that I could go back to those memories and really sit with the feelings and have empathy for myself as someone who is trying their best and who was just doing the best that they could. An example is in my book I write about this time in which I was hanging out with a bunch of people, and they were all mostly queer people of color with really rad politics who I met through protests and stuff. I wanted so badly to be liked that when this cis gay white dude made an offhanded Islamophobic comment about how he's so glad to be talking to me because otherwise he would have avoided the religious person in the room. . . . That has always stayed with me because my response in that moment was to almost have a fawning response, and make myself be one of the good ones and just be super friendly or just not call him out on that. I just really wanted him to like me and that's always stayed with me as a moment that I felt really ashamed because I thought, "Oh my God, I can't believe I did that."

LAMYA: Being able to write about it and put myself back in that moment where I was a young person, looking for community, looking to find other people, looking to make friends, to have empathy with myself and realize that I learned so much from that moment—that I would never do that again. There was something about that, that in retrospect felt both really healing and felt like I could have empathy for myself. So that was something that was really surprising to me. People talk about writing books as cathartic—I'm reading this really gorgeous book right now called *Feeding Ghosts* which is all about healing through writing and healing a mother-daughter relationship through writing. I guess I totally missed that writing could do that. And so it was such a beautiful, pleasant surprise to be able to experience that through the act of writing.

KHADIJA: Wow. Finding a community is a lot of trial and error. I also remember being in this community and also wanting so bad to be liked and just letting things slide. So I like what you said about having empathy for yourself, because you're kind of in a shock and then you think about it later and you're like, "Oh my gosh, this was a terrible thing that happened to me." And sometimes acknowledging that other people also have to speak up too when they hear things like that.

LAMYA: I really want that on a T-shirt or a bumper sticker: "community is trial and error."

KHADIJA: Yes! Let's write that down!

LAMYA: You'll design those!

KHADIJA: Yes, ha-ha! Towards the end of the memoir you talk about modesty in regard to your hijab and describe it as your beard around your family. Has your view changed since then or could you describe that kind of defense a little bit more?

LAMYA: Yeah, yeah. It's interesting because one of the most popular reasons why I think men tell women to wear hijab is this whole idea of modesty and that in and of itself has never really appealed to me as a concept. Like what does that even mean? Like why do women have to be the receptacle of this concept that feels so weird and tied to purity whereas men don't. So that's never really been a big reason for me in terms of why I wear the hijab. It is really important to me because it's aspirational towards a relationship with God. It's just this constant reminder that, "I am this person who is doing this because I want this guiding principle of a God and therefore justice to really form the cornerstone of how I live my life." One of the things that feels like a double-edged sword in terms of wearing a hijab is the way that it becomes this beard in terms of queerness. I'm talking about a beard in that sense of that word where people would have these fake relationships with men, and they were their beards so that they passed as straight, or that they could hide their queerness when they needed to. It's really interesting to me the ways that hijab does that for me—when I'm around family, or when I'm at my mosque, or I'm in situations where I'm not talking about my queerness. Because I wear a hijab, people just assume that I'm straight. It's like this double-edged sword because I think there's this way in which people tend to read hijab in an automatically feminine way. Although people are really pushing back against that on the Internet. All these young people, butch hijabis and masc hijabis on TikTok and Instagram. I don't know if you've seen them, but it's so adorable.

LAMYA: So it's really interesting because on one hand, it sort of protects me where I don't necessarily want to announce my queerness. But what feels hard is that it also genders me in a particular way that doesn't always feel true. So that's something that I grapple with a lot with hijab. As I think more about my gender and really come into being non-binary, I've begun to wear a hijab in different ways. Like sometimes I will wear a scarf, but sometimes I'll wear a baseball cap—a backwards baseball cap or a beanie. To me, those practices feel deeply continuous, it feels like other ways of wearing a hijab.

KHADIJA: I've seen those videos where people are wearing their alternate hijabs or they're more masc. And I've been exposed to that so much because that's some of the stuff that I build my social media timelines and stuff around me on. So I'm like, "wow, they're so cool!" It does feel like kind of a feminine thing that people who aren't exposed to hijabis just gravitate toward and expect. We already touched on the community a little bit already but for me, it's kind of hard to get that. I'm in a small town in the Midwest and it's a college town. So the bigger cities around me have masjids, but I still have to drive 45 minutes—which isn't a problem—but I would like to have something much closer. The part of your book that talks about making friends at the LGBTQIA mixer really gave me hope. What did it feel like for you to find this community?

LAMYA: Honestly, it saved my life, and I don't say that lightly. I feel like I don't know who I would have been if I wasn't able to find queer Muslim community. I feel really, really lucky. I live in New York—the best city in the world—but what I love about New York is that you're never the weirdest person in the room. There's so many people from all over, geographically and in terms of identity, and I feel really, really lucky to have found queer Muslims. And it wasn't until I found queer Muslims who were all living differently, who were living their queerness and their Muslimness in different ways. There are some people who didn't necessarily identify as Muslim or identified as Muslim-ish or culturally Muslim. And then there were people who were just living their queerness in different ways too. Just watching people navigate that and be authentically themselves gave me permission to do the same. Honestly, I feel so, so, so lucky.

LAMYA: I know that a lot of people are building virtual communities. There's all of these Muslim orgs that are trying to do a lot more, and do local and national work. So, it's pretty cool to see that. I know MASGD is doing a lot of virtual programming, Queer Crescent also does a lot of cool things. But just being able to find community really changed my relationship to queerness, to Islam, and it just taught me so much. I feel so, so, so grateful to have found the people I did.

KHADIJA: That's amazing. So, what do you say to people who are incredibly stuck on the contradiction between—or I guess their idea of the contradiction—between being Muslim and being queer. Like, what do you do? How do you navigate those conversations? Have you had them recently?

LAMYA: Honestly, I try to avoid them because to me, it just feels like a losing premise, you know what I mean? It feels like it starts from this place of assumptions and baggage, whereas the queer Muslims that I know are just living their truths. They're living their queerness, they're living their Muslimness in whatever way it works. To me, the thing with contradictions and messiness is that it's generative, I think it causes you to live life in ways that are intentional and beautiful. And at the end of the day, that's what I want out of life: to live with some sort of fight towards justice or fighting towards justice with a real thoughtfulness.

KHADIJA: You're very vocal on your Instagram page about your support for Palestinians and I appreciate that. Can you talk about your support? I saw that you did a collaboration with Books for Palestine and how they donated money to Gaza. Or maybe something else that you're doing or have done that has brought attention to Palestine.

LAMYA: In my non-Lamya life I've been organizing, so I feel like I can't really talk about it. But with my alter ego, I feel like all I can do is boost the news and fundraisers. I don't have a good answer to this question, but I feel very helpless, as do we all. I don't quite know how to navigate it as a writer besides just posting as much as I can. One of my friends has this life goal which I think is really beautiful, which is every time you're given a mic, make sure to talk about Palestine, which I think is just a really important thing. So I've been trying to do that every time I have an interview or a podcast. I find some way to mention it, just so that it's always on people's minds. If it can cause one more person to read more about it, I think that that's something.

KHADIJA: Yeah. And everything feels like it's not enough.

LAMYA: Oh my god, yes, totally.

KHADIJA: Sometimes even having conversations, it's like you just keep talking about it but every day is something new, so I get that helpless feeling.

KHADIJA: We kind of talked about this, but do you see a shift in the culture towards more progressive views from Muslims or do you think the community is becoming more accepting of queerness, or if not, what do you think that some of these setbacks are?

LAMYA: I don't know, I may be off, but the sense that I get is that there seems to be this real bifurcation. It seems like so many younger folks are really chill about queerness, about gender, and are exploring those things for themselves. And then I also see this reactiveness towards that which feels really frustrating and also mirrors the way that right-wing movements have been pushing back against transness and queerness in really violent ways, in systemic ways. I was talking about this yesterday so it's really on my mind. I've been thinking a lot about the "navigating differences" open letter thing, do you know what I'm talking about?

KHADIJA: I don't think so, no.

LAMYA: It was this awful open letter that a whole bunch of imams and leaders in the community wrote, I think about maybe a year or a half ago. It reads like right-wing propaganda and the basic gist of it says that we as Muslims shouldn't have to be okay with queerness, we shouldn't have to be okay with transness. That it's against the way that we practice our faith and we shouldn't have to learn about queer history in schools, we shouldn't have to be surrounded by this, and "this is wrong in Islam." Which is so fucked up because that's not even true and what does that even mean? Honestly, it felt like right wing talking points if you read it. I think I was just really, really frustrated and angry at that in ways that a lot of people were. A lot of imams who signed it were sort of like big names with big followings in some parts of big Islamic centers. So that was really, really, really frustrating and really enraging. I'm hopeful that people can sort of see through that because it's just really, really fucked up.

KHADIJA: Yeah, it feels more like the people within my generation or our generation are paving way for acceptance and love. Every time I go home, my parents are like, "Are you still married to that woman?" I'm like, "Yes, she's not my friend the way you guys thought she was!" But then you have to remember that they're your parents. They're aunts. They're grandparents and these ideas are kind of fizzling out from them, but it's still within mosques and in churches and it's still very isolating sometimes.

LAMYA: Right, exactly. That's so cute though, how long have you guys been together?

KHADIJA: We've been together for four years and we got married last September. So I totally get what you say when you have to go to your family and be like, "Yeah, this is my roommate, this is my best friend." And she was so confused by that. She was like "My parents accept me, why can't yours?" And having to remember I was raised in an African Muslim household, we can't do that here. So navigating that was pretty hard.

KHADIJA: I saw you're currently writing a book called *99 Names for God*, and I love the title. I know you probably can't give out too much information. Is there a process for writing that you have for this that's different from your memoir or is it kind of the same?

LAMYA: Honestly, I'm not even kidding when I say that with my first book, I feel like I kind of lucked into it. I wrote it over the course of a couple of years and the shutdown was happening then and I couldn't do my nine-to-five job because that required being in person. And so, all I was doing during the shutdown was writing and it just felt like it kind of happened to me. Whereas with this book, I feel like I have to really be really disciplined about it. I also have a kid now and so that makes finding time to write really difficult. So I feel like I need a writing practice now, which is something that I've been working on in ways that I didn't when I was writing my first book. I describe the act of writing my first book as like having a crush—all you want to do is find time and write. Where now I have to be like, "Okay I have 45 minutes and I'm waiting at the doctor's office. What if I took my computer and wrote over there for a little while?" I have to find pockets. I've had to really develop a writing practice. I've always written in a community, but it's become really important with writing this book because community really helps keep me accountable to word goals or time goals or applying for grants. So it's been a real shift in ways that feel really cool. I get to do this disciplined and more thoughtful writing practice.

KHADIJA: You mentioned writing groups. I'm sure there's a plethora of them in New York, but how is it? I don't think we have many of those here unless you go to the university, but what is that like?

LAMYA: Honestly, I've been finding a lot of writers and then pulling them into a writing group with me. So I think it can also be a matter of finding people and then just like making them do it with you. But it's been really, really lovely. I was also really lucky to take a class in New York, a writing class called "Two Truths and a Lie," which if you're interested in... I tell everyone to do this because it's virtual and it's just a gorgeous class by Bushara Rahman, who wrote this book called *Roses in the Mouth of the Lion*. Have you heard of this book?

KHADIJA: I have not, but I will write it down.

LAMYA: It is such a beautiful book and it's about growing up as a Pakistani immigrant in the 80s in New York. It's very steeped in geography and very steeped in the 80s and it's just such a beautiful book. I didn't do an MFA and most of the people who come are not people who are in MFA programs, although there are some that are. It's a mixture of craft and generative problems and meeting and finding communities. So I was able to find a community there. I went to the Lambda Literary retreat a few years ago, which I'm also a huge fan of. That's also virtual this year. And it's just this gorgeous space where people can come, learn skills, workshop pieces, and just really get a lot out of. So I found a community through that as well. I think the coolest thing about a writing community is that when it works, it's just glorious for accountability, for an audience. So, I've been really, really enjoying that.

KHADIJA: Yeah, I sometimes forget that people can put on virtual writing workshops. I always feel like you have to do it at a coffee shop, but it's just so hard to get people's schedules and get them out of the house. That's really cool, though.

KHADIJA: Last question: what is the last or current book that you read, can you talk about it, and what it's doing for you right now?

LAMYA: I actually just finished reading this about an hour ago on the train. It's called *Feeding Ghosts* and it's a graphic memoir by Tessa Hulls and it is so beautiful. I've been on this real reading roll where the last maybe five or six books that I read I've been blown away by and this was just so beautiful. It actually recently won the Pulitzer for autobiography/memoir. So, it's definitely worth checking out. It traces this grandmother, mother and daughter through history and talks about China and the various takeovers and regimes that have happened in the last, I guess, 80 years and the trauma that was passed down from one generation to another especially through migration and immigration, it's just so beautiful. I think I'm going to be recommending this to everyone.

KHADIJA: Yeah, that sounds really beautiful, I love graphic novels. I don't think I've ever read a graphic memoir, but graphic novels are just amazing to see play out. I'll have to add that to my list.

LAMYA: Yeah, definitely check it out.

KHADIJA: So is there anything else that you wanted to say or touch up on?

LAMYA: No, I think that's it. But thank you for these really beautiful questions.

IFTAH YAH SIMSIM

Amal Ishaque

In the streets of Al Nasiriyah
or was it Al Nassriyah?
Nasriyaah?
Bhai jaan, do you remember the bougainvillea vine
escaping our spiked garden wall?

The only son in the family
after maghrib you walked to the corner store
for freshly baked bread

What was it called Bhai jaan?
I forget
honeyed whole wheat
soft and warm like Ammi's face on the days she chose to smile

They chased you as you ran home
the same boys hurled stones at us
with the righteousness of the permitted
"Hindi baba go home!"

Bhai jaan, I still wonder
who is Hindi Baba?
Did they mean Hindu babu?
Or bibi?

I imagine her as one of many nannies
beating wings against a marble drenched House of Saud

days spent living just outside the frame
a body with temporary papers
never quite in focus

Does she send back remittance payments
wrapped in endearments to her children?
meri pyari beti meri jaan

Do they screen her mail?
redact truth
continue to claim she's "part of the family"

Bhai jaan, wasn't there an Oum Kulthum ballad
about a woman lost?
Or was it Fairuz?

Remember how they always played those old songs on TV
between Arabic Sesame Street
"Iftah ya Simsim abwabak, nahn-ul-atfaal..."

and the evening news
which never mentioned the Filipina maids
found dead at a construction site in downtown Riyadh
or the stoning of that woman in chop chop square
we stumbled across when shopping in the souk

I can't understand the songs anymore Bhai jaan

Despite Mrs. Leila's daily school beatings
the letter ayn still wants to catch in my throat
my tongue a rebellion against the Arabic they forced us to learn

Bhai jaan
memories ghost by
trailing faint traces of blossoms
from the orange tree in the corner

I cannot remember
when exile became home

LANGUAGE

Amal Ishaque

The language of foreign remittances
was the first tongue I spoke

Do not then judge me
if I need translation
to understand
the ghazals of my ancestors

GEN·O·CIDE / DISJOINTED

Eva Roslin

"What are you going to do about it?"

Holy mountains,
Stolen.
So much land,
Taken.
Burning women on crosses,
Forsaken.

Beheaded,
hanged,
they spit on our corpses,
pulled out our unborn children,
slick with viscera,
torn out of mother's stomachs like calves,
babes who would never taste mother's milk.

Smyrna engulfed in fire.
Diyarbakir and Adana drowning in blood,
red pools seeping down to the roots,
making rotten trees grow over bones.

Deserts with sand that burned flesh.
No water, no savior.
Corpses everywhere.
Children who could no longer go on.

"Who will believe you?"

Marched out of trains,
Heads shaved,
poison streams,
a chorus of screams.
The murderers among the Reich...inspired

"Who, after all, remembers the Armenians?"

Cemetery full of lingering lives,
trapped in the walls.
The murderers scrub over and again,
but the spirits stay watching.

Images don't die.
You cannot erase us.
The archives are a testimony of your lies,
archives you control without reprise.
We know what you did.
We will shout until our voices are scraps,
whispering in the shadows.

"What are you going to do about it?"

ARTIST STATEMENT FOR *TETAS'TEARS (QUEER TATREEZ)* AND *ZAHRI MOON WITH FEATHERS (QUEER TATREEZ)*

Micaela Kaibni Raen

We are not numbers on the news. We are Queer/Trans Palestinians, and SWANA Dykes, and our love transcends empire.

Tetas' Tears (Queer Tatreez) is dedicated to Queer/Trans Palestinians and Southwest Asian/ North African (SWANA) Queer/Trans women, Dykes, and sapphic folk. Whether living on ancestral homelands or surviving diasporic exile, many of us struggle against our own erasure while still dreaming new futures.

I live in exile occupying Indigenous lands not my own. My exile manifests as profound grief for those my presence displaces and a fierce dedication to North American Indigenous sovereignty through Land-Back activism.

My own diasporic transplantation is a dislocating cognitive dissonance, a disruptive static fragmenting memory, eyes clouded by shrouds piling heavy loss after loss, a skeleton key that opens a door lost to rubble long ago, an endless consumption of mournings' shocking stings, and an insatiable rage longing for home.

I am my grandmother's dream, and she is mine. We exist together through Tatreez, Indigenous Palestinian textiles and embroidery. Traditionally Tatreez, and knowledge of its creation, have been passed down Palestinian female to Palestinian female. As the culture of Tatreez evolves within our Palestinian communities so does its inclusivity to diverse genders and sexualities. However, I must acknowledge a vital truth. . . . Queer/Trans Palestinians have always created, shared and celebrated Tatreez.

Although the focus of *Tetas' Tears (Queer Tatreez)* is Palestinian Tatreez, many SWANA regions have traditions of designing and celebrating embroidery and stitched textiles. Embroidery, while unique to each community, has also acted as a communicative language across SWANA lands for many generations. There has been cultural exchange through the sharing of specific motifs, stitching patterns, thread colors, and evolving techniques. In this way, *Tetas' Tears (Queer Tatreez)* continues our legacy of artistic communication and strives to be a looking glass in which we can come together, as SWANA Dykes, and see ourselves.

As a Palestinian lesbian artist, I feel Tatreez holds intricate insights and connectivity to Indigenous femininities that can be accessed through the patterns, repetitions, and mathematical matriarchal matrices inherent in stitching sequences. My goal is to discover these insights and create a new visual artform, *Queer Tatreez*. A style of art and literature focused on ancestral wisdom that embraces Queer/Trans Palestinians and the land that gives us life.

For this artwork, I researched ancient and modern patterns of Palestinian embroidery to plot and re/create the background design digitally one stitch at-a-time. The Tatreez motif shown has many names including "Moon with Feathers" and has many interpretations. The pink galaxy of stars behind the stitching refers to the divine feminine energy that brings us connection and re/birth. The stitches were placed in a larger context with hand drawn and painted elements. Once the centered portions were completed, the textile images were placed cascading down the sides, composing a vertical frame.

In this work, teta is represented as a spiritual compilation of grandmothers. Her image has two faces looking both backward and forward in time. Both timelines show her grief as tears and her tears are represented by kite shapes. One face showcases the Tatreez patterns on her skin while the other does not. Even when not visible the embroidery pattern is still present, emphasizing the strength and importance of Tatreez as a cultural and spiritual inheritance. Tetas' mouths are closed to reflect the global climate of racist ethnic/cultural erasure and the blatant censorship of Palestinian and SWANA voices.

The kite imagery is meant to be a heartfelt testament to Gazan children; including those who have been targeted, imprisoned, and killed. In 2011, the children of Gaza were awarded the Guinness World Record for the most kites flying simultaneously.

The kites in rainbow colors symbolize the tears of Queer/Trans Palestinians and SWANA Dykes suffering, many without basic human rights, under violent racist and homophobic colonial regimes. The tears act as our archive compiling our stories across time while honoring those who are missing, imprisoned, or have been murdered.

The larger kite/tears are shown in the colors of the Palestinian flag. With little documentation and no headstones, these tears are our death markers, re/telling the stories of the families killed during the ongoing Nakba in Palestine. This is in direct reference to whole families (complete genetic lines of familial relatives) that have been attacked and assassinated. Especially targeted were the families of teachers, leaders, medical workers, activists, journalists, authors, service workers, and so many more. Statistics show that death in Palestine disproportionately silences children, women, and those working toward health and justice. In addition, the larger kites resemble feathers to honor the plight of migrating birds, and the loss of their habitats, as they are being devastated by vast ecocides affecting SWANA countries caused by militarized colonialism.

Contemplating Palestinian Tatreez patterns, and the act of its creation, become a powerful bridge to my grandmothers, where I sit in our sacred Tatreez Circle, embraced, and listen.

Tatreez our transcendent hoop
spiraling r/evolutions
continuances
resistances
threading tears in poppies' skies
our enduring
a tale in sewn motif
here I claim
my knotted stitching
my pages in our stories
may we be stitched into cloth
with Queer and Trans Palestinian ancestors
who have always been
and always will be
woven patterns within patterns
a calculation of

sky to earth
star to moon
leaf to wind
needle to thobe
then to now
a textiled bridge
our timeless embrace
without whose formulaic computations
we would not exist

JEALOUSY

Sarah E. Azizi

For Madi

an untended garden

thick vines choke
budding flowers

petals scatter

dogs trample tulips
leave roots in tatters

it's sticky, sickly sweet
the soil's sour

& all you have to do
is tend the garden but

all you have to do
is tend the garden

AMERICAN DAMAGES

Sarah E. Azizi

On even the best days, the anxious
thoughts creep in: what if today
is the last good day? What if the news

isn't same old, & the world tilts
until each axis cracks? Exile is cold
but familiar. You can't expect more

of me. I was 22 months old
when I was hurried from one part
of the world to another. The shoe's

always mid-drop. One day I fell in love,
another he started yelling at me
and wouldn't stop. My heart knows

best the drum beat of belonging
to warring parties: the longed-for
lover a pariah too dangerous to visit,

lest I not be allowed to leave; the other an angry
husband who confuses ownership
w/ love, believes that might makes right, always

sorry too late to reverse the damage done.

MAKE A WISH

Sarah E. Azizi

This lemon-soaked raspberry fits
the tip of my tongue like a little
hat. The heat of my mouth forces it
to melt, sweet & tangy. French roast
coffee slides down my throat. I turn
my face to the window, soak up
the warmth of the September sun.
It's so quiet. I'm scrolling.
The lit screen disturbs my tableau
of simple things, but I can't help myself.
I'm seeking advice, just a dollop. Tell me how
to cast off my well of begrudging sighs.
My plants thrive, the happy puppy circles
my feet. I stretch my toes. Such silence
before my child wakes, almost sensual
how it embraces me. With everyone,
I teeter between joyously, lovingly
welcoming, & put upon, annoyed. Resentful.
This quality I detest most in myself;
too, how unpredictable I remain, even to me,
nearly half a century in. One day, I remind
myself, there will be no dog or child;
just you, maybe a plant or two ...
My daughter's feet stomp above.
The counter of dishes admonishes,
piled high w/ the chore she abandoned,
per the usual, last night. I imagine
the counter clear, sink holding only

my cup & spoon, all of it pristine.
Will it be soothing, the simplicity
of a life that's all my own,
or will I spend it yearning for her fist
pounding until the flatware & glasses clatter,
her passion getting ahead of her, like me,
she the glistening apple of my tree?
Whatever's coming—peace & solace,
a fertile bed for my creativity, or longing
& emptiness, a hollow womb howling—
I'll find out soon enough. For now, more coffee
& a caress for the dog. My child's voice
disrupts the silence. I tune mine & call back,
arrange my countenance to show her, truly,
it is no pantomime, she is the most wondrous
being in the world. What I wish for her:
the sublime, secure pleasure of the single
cup & spoon. The tremendous feeling
of being untethered, & the certainty of being
sewn up within. What I imagine, rather,
it would feel like to know & trust, mind
to gut, in every cell, that you are whole,
that you yourself are a complete expression
of being. And if I get a second wish, it is
for her well to be so deep, she never stumbles
thru a shallow part, falls & flails, sputters
decades into nothingness. In real time,
her feet move from stairs to landing.
Morning, Madi. Hungry? The glass bowl
of red berries trembles in my hands.
Her fingers seek out one, & place
the tender fruit on the tip of her tongue.

STICKERS

Noor Al-Dayeh

Media: Photograph   Photo Credit: Noor Al-Dayeh

ANOTHER SAD ARAB DYKE POEM

Noor Al-Dayeh

I wish I had a partner
That I could
Make tea for
And
Buy flowers and
Make playlists (like. . . so many playlists)
And
Take on dates
And give dates to!
And Kiss
And
And Call Hayati
And
And, And, And!!!!
But instead
I'm in handcuffs on 55th & 5th
Yelling in the lobby of fuck ass
Trump Tower
Unable to be on Tinder
Or
Be normal at a bar Or
Whatever the fuck normal dykes do
I wish I had a partner
Who would've been there for me
As jail support
Instead
I rode home on the Q alone
Another sad Arab Dyke <3

EROTIC LABOR UNION

Melina McConatha

thirsty for erotic community care

my sex work as skilled labor,
a survival tool swap
for an embodied life

grief, rage, pleasure

a deep pussy's path to ancestors
where my great great grandmothers ghost
smokes a pipe and serves the tea
an ancient form of mutual aid

we rewild community care
spit solidarity
choke on power

our discipline in movement,
a flock of birds
on a current of resistance

for abolition
for land back
for queer rest

tides under a new moon
cum for us
to begin again

BLOOD MONEY

Andrea Abi-Karam

ride my face
to Barbara
Hammer
i say
b/w
blood
soaked
walls
& her
film
reel
of
flowers
/ pubes
the gq
bathroom
built by
the same $$
architecting
gen0cide
a refrain
i refuse
w/ each
breath
b/w
drops

COUNTERPULSE

Andrea Abi-Karam

the night after Sister Spit tour wrapped, i took BART into the city to give a performance as part of counterpulse fest, opening for Valerie Reding a swiss dancer, makeup genius, general artist freak from Zurich i had met a couple of years earlier and we had worked together on a show. she had asked me to open for her, the lead saturday night performance of the two week festival. feeling particularly fearless post-tour, i did most of my makeup before getting on the train drawing wires around my eyes and down my face for a cyborg effect. someone on the train tried to strike up conversation with me after staring for several minutes, i did my best to be polite and tried to keep it short. i got off at the montgomery stop and noticed he was following. the montgomery station wasn't that big and i tried to lose him unsuccessfully while my heart raced. counterpulse was only a couple of blocks away but i was terrified if i walked i wouldn't make it. i had pepper spray on me, unclipped it from my keys and clutched it knuckle white in my hand. i could probably outrun him, but what if i took a wrong turn and couldn't find the venue—it had been awhile since i'd been to counterpulse. swiftly i weighed the risks and opted to find a cab. SF wasn't new york, it wasn't always easy to find a cab. but downtown SF was a better bet than other neighborhoods. i knew from pedicabbing that they sometimes hung around the hotels a block up from the station. i ran up the station stairs and up towards the hotels still seeing him out of the corner of my eye in pursuit.

i ducked around the hotel valet area and hopped in a cab and locked the door. as calmly as i could manage i said HI. I'm Being Followed. Can You Take Me To Counterpulse? It's Just Around The Corner. I Know But I'm Being Followed, Please Feel Free To Circle Around A Few Times, I Want To Make Sure We've Lost Him. You're Really Being Followed? Yes ! Let's Go! he gunned the cab out of the line and away from this quagmire of pursuit. i wondered how i was being perceived in this moment. a scared girl with an overactive imagination? a young gay boy hustler being chased by an unhappy customer? a tourist who had no idea where they were going? and what about on the train? was the staring one of simultaneous disgust and attraction? had he given up his own dreams of being an artist for a nasty drug habit and tendency to stalk and murder any reminders of that old ambition? was his plan to assault me into being cis? yell at me about 911? steal my leather jacket and sell it for meth? whatever it was, it was creepy, and after two weeks of being part of a roving pack of QTPOC performers, i suddenly felt very alone and without defense. the cost of visibility in this moment manifested as severe.

drea and diesel were meeting me there i had put them on the list for my performance. i texted drea and told her what had just happened, that i was freaked out. she said she'd be there in 20 and was glad i got a cab. the cab wrapped around a hot corner of the tenderloin where counterpulse was dropped in as an obvious marker of artist based gentrification, enjoying affordable, or formerly affordable cheap rent in a historically low income neighborhood of sex workers, queers, drugs. the cab pulled up in front of the big glass window of the venue and said

How's This? i looked around and didn't see anyone trailing around. i asked if he would wait until they let me inside, They Lock The Doors Until It's Time For The Show and tipped him 50%. Ok, he said. i slid out of the cab and knocked on the door. at first i didn't see anyone and my heartbeat quickened. what if i was too early? is that even possible for a show that has a proper tech time? before long a staff unlocked the door and let me in, while standing in the glass frame of the doorway i looked over my shoulder and nodded at the cab and mouthed Thanks before he sped off. the staff showed me to a corner in the foyer right outside the main black box which was to be my stage. Do You Want To Test the Projector? Yeah, Sure, Thanks. i climbed over a line of what looked like wooden under the bed storage containers that segmented the corner from the rest of the room. their projector was powerful, glitching light cascaded off the wall, the ceiling, my high alert body still yet to drain the adrenaline from being pursued by a strange man in downtown san francisco. This Is Perfect, i said, Thanks. Is There Somewhere I Can Get Ready? i needed a minute and wanted to check on my makeup. Yes, There's a Green Room, I'll Take You Over There. Thanks, i said. the staff led me through a subterranean labyrinth of narrow, bright white hallways before arriving at the green room filled with mirrors, make up, wigs, costume trunks, bright vanity lights and of course a cooler with seltzer and beer.

as my the vibrations of my skin began to slow and synch with the rest of my body i looked in the mirror intended for drag queens, actors, and performers to rearrange their appearances for the stage. i thought about how so much of my identity is wrapped up in being aggressively visible, reflective. how i saw makeup and fashion and studs as extensions of the visceral adornments of simultaneous visibility and defense. leather was a second skin, literally. studs were repellent, literally. most people did not like getting glitter on them and did not want to touch me, but of course they wanted to stare. i considered how all of this had led to me being followed by a creepy man. what was the suggestion of this experience? to tone it down? dull my shine? blend in with the sea of venture capital funded app brand logo hoodies? with the adrenaline wearing off i began to feel nauseous and grabbed a crisp seltzer from the green room cooler. i was here to perform a long antifa poem that i had adapted for performance before Sister Spit tour. i was here to confront the conditions of rising new fascism in the US and implicate the audience until they felt urged to rise above complicity and *do something*. i was here to shine, spike, command the energy of the room. i was here to staple myself.

FASCISTS ARE NICE

WIDAD

EDITORS' NOTE: WIDAD wrote this piece in July 2024 during the 2024 U.S. presidential election season. As of April 2025, an estimated 680,000 people have died in Gaza since October 2023. This includes deaths due to imposed deprivation.[1]

Malcom X once said that "the white liberal differs from the white conservative only in one way: the liberal is more deceitful than the conservative."

Since 2023, the white liberals of America have sent billions of dollars of tax-funded weapons to a genocidal apartheid state that is slaughtering, displacing, and starving millions of innocent civilians in the overpopulated and besieged ghetto we call the Gaza Strip.

Wrapping themselves up in the illusion of decency, white liberals rest comfortably on stolen land while pontificating about LGBT and women's rights—as if queer Palestinians aren't starving in Gaza; as if Israeli soldiers aren't raping Palestinian women in arbitrary detention. Gay Israeli reservists raise the pride flag over the rubble of Palestinian homes while the liberal New York Times publishes an article about how Israeli women are "making history" fighting on the frontlines of Gaza.

1 *Skewering History: The Odious Politics of Counting Gaza's Dead by Dr. Richard Hill and Dr. Gideon Polya.*

As a queer feminist, I can confidently say that breaking the glass ceiling does not include crushing the bodies of innocent children under the weight of their own homes.

Palestinians know that while Israel may be executing this genocide, it is ultimately the United States that is committing it. Liberals continue to vilify Republicans even though it is the Democrats that have unapologetically waged war on international law and human rights. It should come as no surprise that morality and humanitarianism are outfits that Empires wear until it no longer suits them.

For example, once it became clear that Joe Biden was increasingly unfit to govern a world superpower, Democrats skipped their own primaries to prop up Kamala Harris in a demonstration of pure panic. Harris subsequently stepped up to the podium to announce that she was abandoning her own base. As youth across America took to the streets to demand an end to U.S. funding for apartheid and genocide, Harris focused her attention on pro-Israeli moderate Republicans by campaigning with a Cheney.

In an interview with "60 Minutes," she announced that she had a "Glock" in her effort to appeal to the gun-toting right. At the Democratic National Convention, she declared that she would ensure America has "the strongest, most lethal fighting force in the world" to roaring cheers by so-called "progressives."

But Harris is just the icing on the cake. Barack Obama used 10 times the number of drone strikes across the Middle East during his eight-year presidency compared to George W. Bush during the Iraq War. If Bush is considered a war criminal, then what is Obama? Trump's immigration policies were heavily criticized during his first term without any acknowledgement that Obama, to this day, deported more people than any president in American history. Barack Obama has been called an "Angel of Death" and "Deporter in Chief," and yet we are still encouraged to see Democrats as our only hope for a better world.

As cop cities crop up across the country, corporations that fund political campaigns on both sides of the aisle are now shifting their production to the private prison industry. Why, you ask? According to the 13th amendment, "neither slavery nor involuntary servitude, *except as a punishment for crime whereof the party shall have been duly convicted*, shall exist within the United States." Hm. Isn't it funny that the U.S. has the largest number of prisoners worldwide? What an interesting coincidence that mega-corporations have the support of *both* Democrats and Republicans to use free and forced labor to make their products. . . .

While Democrats typically do well to hide their hypocrisy and sweep their war crimes under the rug, this election was different. There was an air of desperation in the Democratic party as they pointed their crooked and bloody fingers at the evil Republicans ruining liberal lives. So much so, that the Democrats attempted to beat Republicans by trying to become them.

You see, the two-party system has reached a critical point of failure.

But let it be known that democracy in America has not failed. It simply never existed. The only thing that has failed is the *illusion* of democracy. Our government is an aristocracy that is puppeteered by corporate lobbyists into ignoring the will of the people for the sake of their bottom line.

Those who understand American history know that there is no such thing as democracy in a country that was built on the pillars of settler-colonialism and white supremacy. It ultimately does not matter *who* sits in the seat of POTUS. What matters is the seat itself and the system it governs.

White liberals hold the *possibility* of fascism over the heads of fearful voters as if they themselves are not fascist. Utterly delusional, they are unable to acknowledge that, at best, their policies are right-of-center on the spectrum of global politics. At worst, they are fascist white supremacists who govern the world's largest military and are arguably proponents of history's most vicious terrorist organization: the United States of America—a country that is uniquely characterized by its brutality.

One million Iraqis here, 60,000 Palestinians there. (The Palestinian death toll was estimated to be at least 186,000 in June 2024 by the Lancet Journal. The total death toll is yet to be confirmed and likely exceeds 500,000.) Collateral damage is unavoidable in the noble pursuit of spreading democracy around the world, right? After all, freedom isn't free. There is a price to be paid, and the currency is our lives.

Martin Luther King Jr. himself said that "many blatant forms of injustice could not exist without the acquiescence of white liberals." The myth that fascism is spread by a pack of blood hungry conservatives, instead of the collective complacency and "polite" racism of white liberals protecting their capital, is the secret ingredient of this diabolical recipe.

Daughter of a Holocaust survivor, Naomi Schulman, wrote that "nice people made the best Nazis . . .they were lovely people who turned their heads as their neighbors were dragged away." The Latin translation of the word nice comes from *nescire*, which means "not know," and *nescius*, which means "ignorant." But what is it called when people *do know* and choose to turn their heads anyway?

Democrats and Republicans alike have exploited Jewish victimhood and weaponized accusations of antisemitism to shield themselves and their genocidal allies from accountability for their crimes against humanity. And as the death toll in Palestine skyrockets, the deafening silence of white liberals has confirmed their allegiance to the steady comforts of Empire. But what can we expect from these nice people?

As the saying goes, scratch a liberal and a fascist bleeds.

تقبرني (TA'BURNI)

Christina Hajjar

Media: Photography/collage Photo Credit: Christina Hajjar

DIASPORA DAUGHTER / DIASPORA DYKE

Christina Hajjar

I bear the fruits and flowers of home.
Habibti sighs, savours her harvest.

Habibti sighs, savours her harvest.
Tells me my blood must smell of roses.

My blood must taste of sun-soaked hedge roses.
Our first gen bodies know light like season.

Ripening abundance always in season.
Her bursting fruit, her fragrant waters.

My bursting fruit, her fragrant waters.
Strawberry patch forearm, my lush takes her.

Strawberries and cream shisha, I taste her.
Macerated femme fruit between tongues.

Gardens and maps out of sweet syrup tongues.
Our young borderless bodies showing me home.

I-11, ISLAMABAD

Diya Abbas

A woman sits alone in her stanza, prays to the mirror.
A jinn falls in love with her figure.
The light is out. Every candle in the house flickers
a warning. Her husband is not home.
In love with the woman of everything.
She makes love to herself. Requests
an AC unit, 3 cherries for lipstick, a collection of Iqbal's.
She married a photograph. Her dark mascara made of
the moon's musket oil. Her eyes impaled by a sculptor's
thumbs.

Saturn's rings inflamed her scarf, hexed & hulled. She
says, my life will begin once I am gone. We return to him
in full. All her pleasures withheld by pleasure.
All her nights spent grinded on her own hip. Her purpose
to vessel a boy.
Born without her nose they pray. However, she is willed
enough to bear her body's consequences. The way prayer
bears our faith.

Nightly on the rooftop, sewing an island of needles
to her own grief. She lives in theirs. When I come to see
her I am too late. With our playlist for when she missed
me. Who stayed up late curled in my legs. She sleeps with
one man tonight. Her dreams growl at my touch. She
hates me. For I made choices.

Withdrew. Passed as a boy. Long enough to stay employed
& offer my retribution. No one wants to marry me.
She is too beautiful.
An unkindness of ravens for hair. Her ghazals of bloodlet.
Her mouth a bullethole desire shot through. I finger the
other side & no blood. Instead a string of infinite prayer beads.

Not even music could bear to remember us. I am asked to
make chai & the pot boils over.
I hand my responsibility to another woman. She resents
me & I thank her. How true she looked on her wedding
day, I imagine. How quickly innocence fluxes in & out the
white sheet hung on the clothesline of our rooftop. In
the wind, I see alternative outlines of her body. Curved &
queered by the lights of another country.

I love you still. I miss the kind of woman you were when
we could touch.

MOSAIC II *A POEM COMPRISED ENTIRELY OF SAPPHO'S FRAGMENTS*

Diya Abbas

For me/ to carry/ the earth/ with her crowns:/
gold anklebone cups./

I would lead/ toward/ you,/ soul beloved,/
around/ these/ roses./ I shall sing beautifully,/

deep sound,/ to gods/ I call out./
For day is near/ and I will pour wine over you.

Earth/ might bestow/ clearsounding/ blame:/
sinful,/ ruinous god,/

swollen/ heart,/ luxurious woman.
I call out/ both you and my servant Eros/

to fight for me./
Songdelighting./

Golder than gold,/ Mythweaver./
But I will not allow you/

to suffer./ Holding the heart/
with hands Persuasion./

I say even in another time/
someone will remember us./

Moon has set/ in her lap/
and Pleiades:/ middle/ spangled/ companions./

O beautiful/ barking tongue./ Sappho, why?/
if/ nothing/ but now/ I want/ to hold/ gold/ Muses.

VALERIAN

Diya Abbas

My obsessions play hide and seek. Another failed metaphor. Nothing guarantees quite like violence. The guilt of running from fire. Ask my family. My longest relationship lasted as long as I could stay. Location determines everything: the page, the sky, two cupped hands. I want to lay all of today's beauty here but no one calls me in the language I grew up with. I blink and the lightning of your teeth is gone. I lean on the walls of the page and demand stillness. I want to gawk the way they gawk at me. Ignoring your last name like a chest. Nothing replicates the eye of the shocked. My failures blink. These things happen everywhere there is language. A woman hovers over a well. History looks like a body of water. I watched friends die without taking them to the sea. Without asking what they loved about skin. Naming them off, another obsession. Naming points fingers at me when the family calls. Language plays in my mother's ears like bells in infinite arrangements. I am not careful enough. A single bullet inside my pillowcase. A single bullet under my forefinger. A single bullet under my tongue. Who will remember love the way it happened. They will say: selfish, always in love with the woman in everything. I say I love you after the poem is over. The final pulp of every animal is an exhalation. The page organized murder. I wrote everyone into a room and handed everyone an empty gun. Said hear.

//

My obsessions play metaphor
nothing like running from my family

as long as the sky stays
I determine today's beauty
everything calls me in lightning.

The page gawks the way they
shock, a woman looks like water.
I watch them without asking and
feel as dead as my friends
naming off another arrangement.

History watched them die without asking
what they loved about a woman.
It happened in the pulp
of a bullet, the rings of ears is a murder.
I remember love as I say it
writing with bells.
I handed my writing
a gun and said exhale.

///

My obsessions play metaphor nothing like relation:
In the well of a woman's eye I cupped the sky

and demanded stillness. Laying on the chest
to the sea. Nothing looks without taking.

I feel alive naming off another bell.
Language arranges history. I remember

guilt as careful bullet. The walls blink
at me when I want her without asking.

Who will love the way I say
love, the way it happened inside

with the woman under my tongue.
The bullet said hear.

I handed my writing
a gun and said exhale.

BUTCH BARED BARITONE

Diya Abbas

"Woman," Woven, Woes of Wonder. Butch
Erratic, Ugly Beauty. Gender-of-Percussion.
Masc of Hands. Masc of Night. Intransitive,
I respond, to your binary negligence
with spit, spent agents, of small pleasure.
Detail of Desire: Hands of pluck & vein.
Sometimes Something you never recognize.
Femme Bait. Femme I Bull, a species of red
Fraction. Apostrophe's Beloved. Barely a Breath
this binder of wire & wounds. I know the flesh
threat of masculinity & the careful disorientations
of woman: the chaotic thrum of heaven's harp heart.
Practice of muscle mouth//Practice of heaven.
My Mother's Mared Steed. My Beloved's praxis of groove.
I put all my bets in my own hands & win:
My valor, my femme, my undeniable steel stars.
Crossbreed, half-fuck, good coin flipped collage
of wrist. Thank God I can never be still:
The space between your eyes blurring into noise.

SAGGITARIUS RISING

AQUARIUS MOON

SAHTEIN!

LIBRA STELLIUM

Nikki Luna

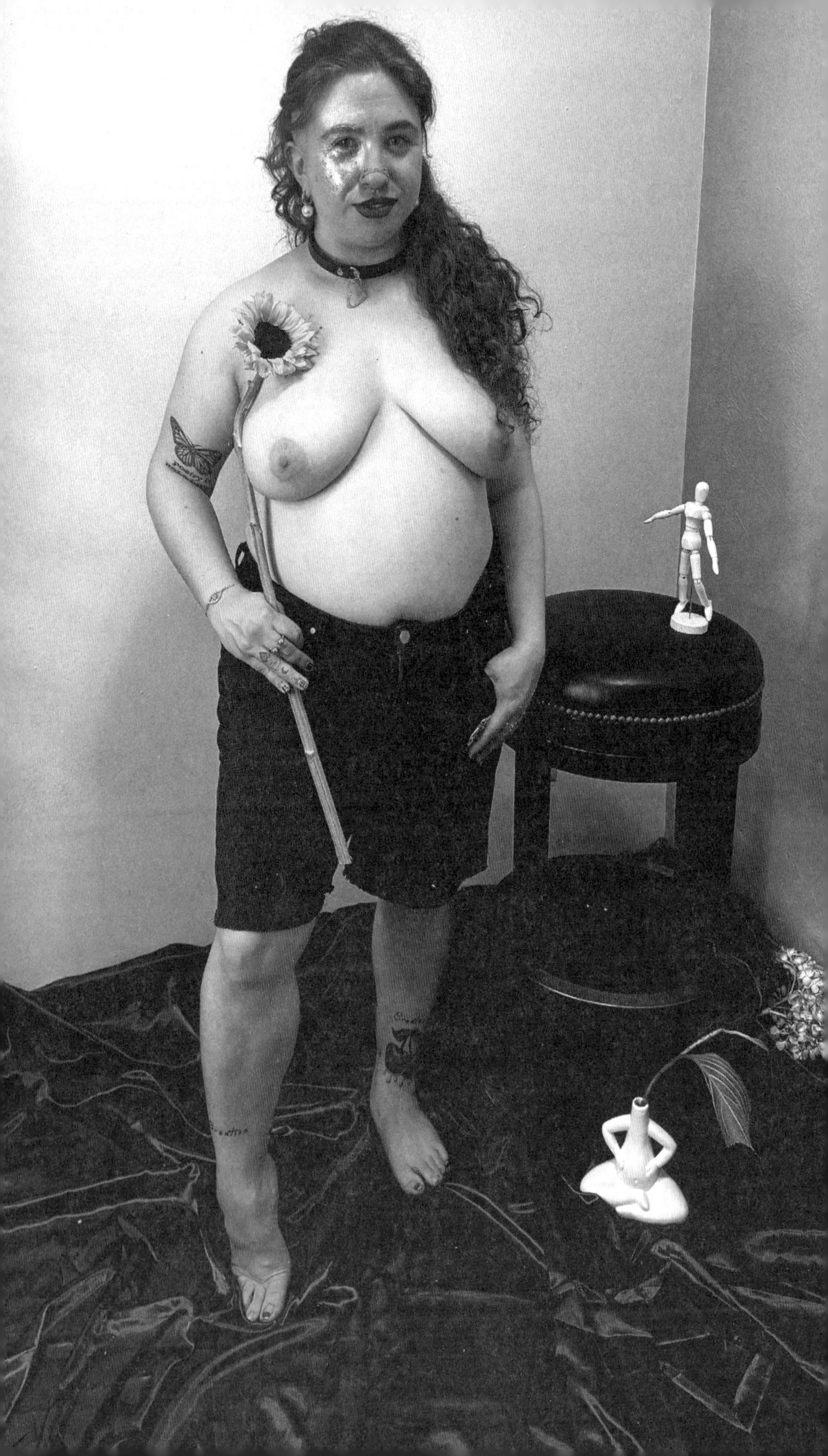

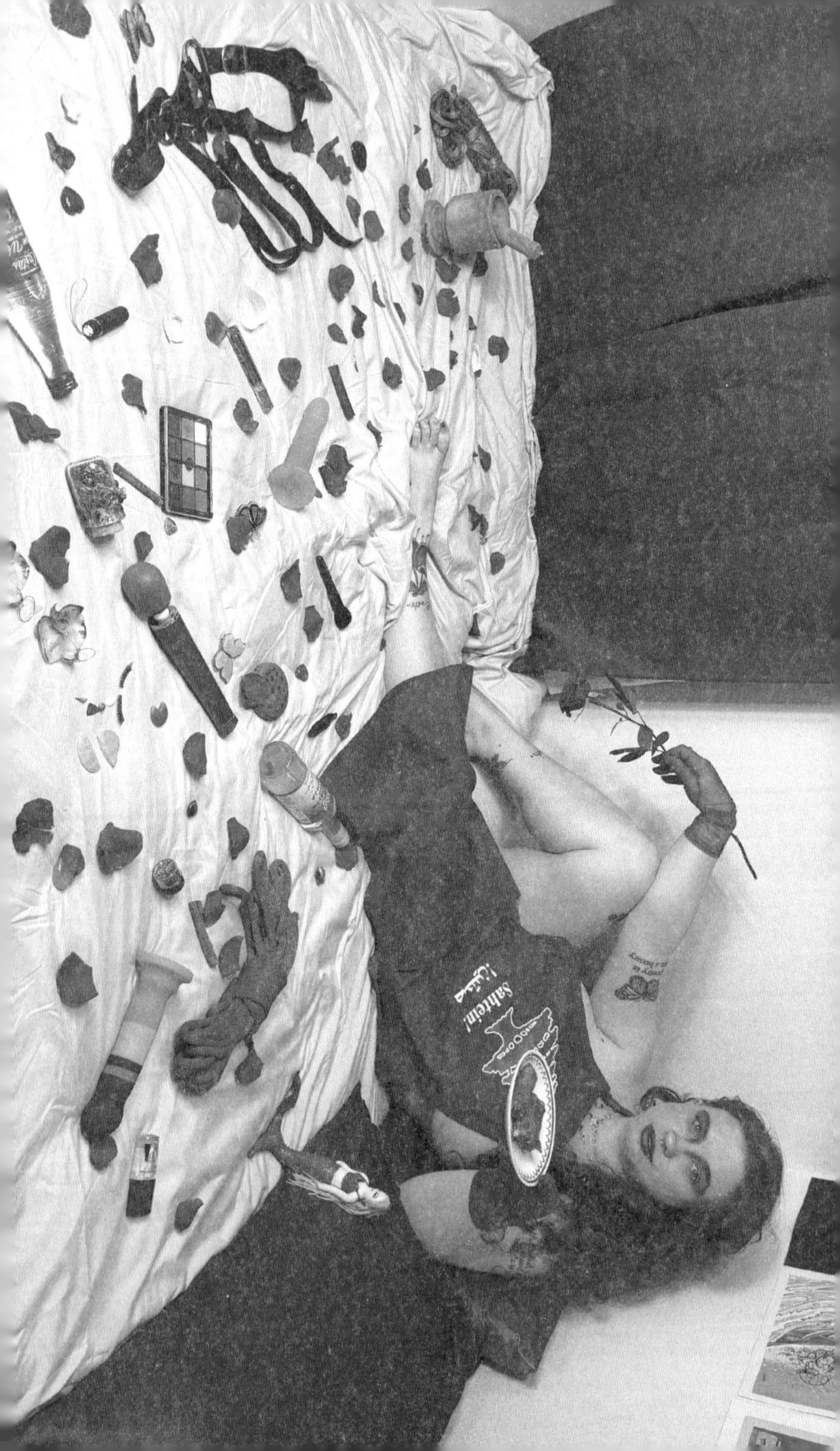
Sahtein!

WOMEN
USED
WE WANT IT ALL
HEAVEN LOOKS LIKE US
PARABLE OF THE SOWER
THE QUEEN OF WANDS
LIFE IS STRANGE
ABOLITION, FEMINISM, NOW.
DESIRE
EYELINER
POETRY AS SPELLCASTING
QUEER TWIN CITIES
Coloring Book

A POETIC NOTICE FROM THE GENDER NON-CONFORMING SPIRIT OF EARTH
FOR JOAN NESTLE

Nikki Luna

NOTICE:

i am the originator of all that
inhabit me
but truthfully in my bitterness

i DO NOT love all.

i am NOT the boundless
never ending yet
bordered & conquerable maiden
those of you who pocket oil & blood stained $$$ desire of me.

i am one in seven hundred quintillion plus planets in the universe!

i generate / lavish / provide beyond a gendered binary

so DO NOT ascribe to me the motherhood of earth
while blazing my skin with white phosphorus.
DO NOT claim a narcissistic national responsibility to
preserve me
while you annihilate bloodlines with bombs
& plot to build settlements on top of tens of millions of
tonnes of legacies and debris.

from my ocean depths i spawned prescient molecules
that collaborated on your eventual design.

i have watched for hundreds of thousands of storied years
while you molded myths about your destined creation.

some of you thought i reside above you

but i have always huddled beneath you
& nestled within you
& morphed alongside you.

i gave life to all

& some of you created a deadly taxonomy.
so many devastating attempts to classify and rank:
sexual paradigms of abnormal & virtuous
gender bindings of determination & functionality
racial castes bolstered by fraudulent sciences & orthodoxies.

to my ungrateful and despicable spawn:
HEAR ME WHEN I SAY
that a land once borderless cannot be stolen
from its caretakers / lives stolen cannot be buried
under hundreds of years of language assimilation /
you cannot line the foundation with riffles /
occupy the clouds with drones /
paint the walls with colonial mythologies /
sweep stolen ancestries into the corner /
wire billions to your proxy /
distribute weapons for profit / for control / for genocides /

& then / look down at the soil / which you soaked in blood /
in oil / in nuclear waste / in fallacies of democracy /
in imported resources /
& be shocked to see / budding / at your feet / the rotting /
glaring / terrifying abomination of a gun violence
epidemic /
whose roots are deep / invasive / and industrialized.

drop your toy submersibles
into my depths

I WILL CRUSH YOU!

pollute my clouds with poison

I WILL MAKE YOU DRINK MY TEAR DROPS!

fly your indignant figureheads
to my sibling mars

THEY WILL SUFFOCATE YOU!

i am your creator

NOT your mother!

i am your creator

NOT your father!

only your mother in the sense
that you were a seed within me
during my own cosmic gestation.

only your father in the sense
that one day my source of energy
will swallow me whole.

i am your creator in the sense
that you came from me
& to me you'll return.

i am your creation in the sense
that you sculpted my horizon
made something fragile / & wounded / out of me.

TAHNĪK

Elias Bouderdaben

Heartache honeys my chest,
    seeps into crevices I had forgotten to shake dust from
as years slip into oblivion
    and age creeps into joints,
    jostling memories and aspirations
scattering them without any regard

My whole life, my mind has
    struggled to make sense of this heart
    and its ache
every day a new understanding; a long-standing nuance

I dream of whispering the adhan in her right ear,
    iqama in the left,
    press the honey to her palate
but after that, it becomes a blur
    windows opaqued with condensation
beads streaking glimpses into possible futures
but mostly the grey of uncertainty

I don't know where
    I will bury her cord

I don't know if a world exists
    that could ever be kind to her

why does the sadness rush to fill my lungs
when I think of the aqiqa we will not have because no one would attend
because she doesn't have a mother and a father
when I think of ramadhans she will not spend in masajid
playing football in the field with the fireflies while the adults pray tarawih

what significance does this sadness hold
what is this heartache asking me to heed
what demons are in this deep desire for this life I want and this life I love
to be safe in a community that has harmed me in ways I'm still learning to name

Will it be possible?

Will I keep her safe?

In my dream, I kiss her left earlobe
whisper
حَيَّ عَلَى الفَلاَح
بسرعة!

the future is waiting for you!

HAYATI

Arielle Zaytoun Sonnenschein

The grapevine planted in our garden has
strength and defiance
it bends the fence under which it was planted
It is slow and stubborn sculpting reality to its
will

I run my hand along the curve rough against
my palm it shows determination what began
as happenstance is now—through choice,
pruning, patience—the divinity of two
hearts meeting over and over a mirage
turned into a marriage

You and I build the dreamworld in a two bedroom palace
filled with apricot walls and a full pantry

The grapes we grow are for comfort and for others—we've
been its shepherd for five years and are rewarded for our care
with warak enab for our beloveds stewed with plump acidic
home grown tomatoes swimming in mint and luxurious
with oil
cooked for the communities we have gifted to each other

The grape leaves are a shelter offering protection
when the unrelenting sun of summer lays its heavy
hand on my shoulder

Hayati you smile in the garden and your neck burns in the
lustrous
daylight your skin warmed like an over ripe strawberry
ready to be
bit

You and I devour the sweet and tannic fruit of a life lived
together
barefoot in the cool clover on a summer night eating hot fruit
laughing at our good circumstances while airplanes circle
overhead beware the ominous angels

In evening we retire with bellies full of contentment
tangled up together like twin vines
radiating heat from the long days, sun

We have learned not all times are good through
unplanned voyages of vast grief visited by autumn and
the silence of winter when the leaves drop off the vine
and the canes are bare we see just how unruly and helpless
everything is we stare at the slender bonelike tendrils frail
and quiet

You hold my hand and I say
'Hayati-it will pass, it must pass'

We cry
the tears are a reservoir of hope for our future
For what will happen next

The silver hairs come in like a diadem upon my head
ordained by many starless nights full of sorrow you
bend to me, kiss my crown and say
'O most glorious and ferocious crone'

Hayati you are
my life
I should like to tend the grapes for fifty years like
a spell and a prayer

may it be so.

CUT-UP FRUIT APOLOGY

Hanan Tuffaha

My mother apologizes after an argument
by cutting up honeycrisp apples and
peaches, placing them neatly on a Dixie
paper plate along with green grapes.
Though her fingers are stiff with arthritis
and I forgot to wash the dishes, hence why
she had to open up the paper china, she still
makes sure I nourish myself.

I know she loves me still despite the fact
she never wanted a lesbian daughter. I wish she
would stop and consider that maybe she
won't be at my wedding, although I will
make sure to send her an invite anyway.
Either way, my mother will make sure I
get my favorite strawberry angel cake, that
she tells the baker about my severe peanut
and tree nut allergy. I hope after I introduce
her to my future fiance, who is not a rich
Arab man, nor a doctor, that she will still
remember I like my peaches soft, with
a dark yellow inside.

BUTTERFLIES

Hanan Tuffaha

After Sappho

I didn't think I was capable of being jealous of a man;
But now I watch his hands gripping your waist
so tightly that the butterflies in my stomach
are replaced with mosquitos.

As his black-painted fingernails dig into your skin,
my gut is overcome with endless red bumps and I am
itching all over.

It's a tingling sort of itch, the kind that gets worse
the longer you try to ignore it.

But all I can do is scratch the bites until they bleed because
swatting the bugs away won't help when
the poison is already on the inside.

When he leans in to place a kiss on your sweet lips...
the same ones that made my body a butterfly sanctuary
the night before,
I ponder how resurrection works.

Meanwhile the mosquitos eat away at what's left of my skin;
the raw and red remnants of flesh,
and I am left to decompose with the butterflies.

BRONI, SHKOL EDI (TAKE MY HAND, MY SON)

Amir Patros

Media: Oil pastel on paper

METAMORPHOSIS

Miqlae

A twister finds its way onto the thobe of a dancer
Girl with red shoes
Throws herself
At love
At indifference
Smashing the porcelain door from which she came
Carves an axe, names it Fate and
Grows into a man who
De-conquered himself
One who
Cut off his feet so he could stand On his own
terms
And named himself
Defiance

HARIQ

Miqlae

touch me with liberation or
handle me like the last candle
when the power is out. position me
like a hero eating his reward
savoring a meal between skies
lustful distractions to weave elaborate lies
I tell myself to feel normal?
happy tears fall from open lips under linen sheets
                in the summer
breath and bone quiver to provoke sleep
the way the ocean gently sways across
the floor of the deep But I still think
about how to protect myself from all the
ways I'm certain you will destroy me

my mouth was made of the sun often
speaks too soon and gives me away
                        as a fire starter

INHERITANCE

Mahru Elahi

Because of Baba's legacy, my notions of family were queer from the start.

Long before marriage, a child, and green cards for birth family, Baba gathered a chosen family together in Illinois. Many were international students, like him. Others were Americans, like the Christian working-class roommate who would spread lard on his toast, or the Jewish kid from Stockton, California who moved back to his hometown after graduation.

Once Baba settled on the West Coast, a family in tow, he tried to visit Stockton every year. Even as body and mind stumbled on the obstacles of age, he drove six hours north from his home in Los Angeles to lace up hiking boots and walk along miles of the Delta Trail with his friend.

Into the empty space of a life far from his politically precarious Iranian birthplace, Baba created something tangible and long-lasting in Amrika.

I wanted to do the same. When I came out to Baba in my twenties—using a xeroxed English-language 'zine distributed by Assal, an informal group for SWANA dykes, as a prop—he was ecstatic.

"Wow. You know what assal means, right?"

"Yes, Baba. We're sweet, like honey. Plus, it's the same word in Farsi and Arabic."

"Are they here, in Los Angeles?"

"Members of Assal come from all over, Baba. Mostly in New York and LA, but also in Minneapolis and Seattle. And other places too, like Europe and Turkey."

"This is great," he said.

We stood shoulder to shoulder as he flipped through the pages. Baba summoned the family names of 'zine contributors into the air between us and guessed at national origin: Iran, Egypt, Lebanon, Afghanistan. His breath smelled faintly of the cinnamon bark he kept lodged between molars.

I leaned my head down, Baba's clavicle pressing against my ear, his chest reaching out and back, out and back, in steady rhythm. I felt like a child again. A child wrapped in the comfort of language and scent.

* * *

There were so many reasons why a federal foster care program, designed to sponsor refugee and unaccompanied youth towards a path to citizenship, became a compelling option for family-building. For one, the program didn't quibble with my queerness, or a name that screamed Islam.

* * *

In 2013, a framed photograph on Sheila's desk caught my eye.

Sheila was a lean woman with brown eyes and a face etched like sandstone, a business manager at the Oakland, California charter school where I had just gotten an offer to teach.

"Wait. You have two teenage daughters?" I said.

The photograph was a family portrait: Sheila and the woman I knew was Sheila's wife—both short of stature, both white—bookended the image. Their arms were entwined with two brown girls who towered over them. All of them smiling at the camera, leaning towards the shutter's click. The two girls were mirror images of one another: long limbs, the same green eyes and unblemished forehead.

"Yes. I convinced my wife to go through with it. She said I'd have to do most of the work," Sheila said.

She wrinkled her eyebrows together and smiled. Sheila's wife had a high-profile job, assisting the superintendent of a large Bay Area school district, while Sheila worked part-time.

"It's hard. The girls have boyfriends and we're not sure what kind of limitations to put on the time they spend unsupervised."

"Ah. High school problems," I said.

"You come from years of high school teaching, right? I should ask you for advice."

I shrugged. "Maybe. How did you end up with the twins?"

"Well, my wife spent a year after college in Sri Lanka and we've always talked about having kids. The civil war ended years ago but so many Sri Lankans were still leaving, particularly young people who lost family. We were already in parenting classes for our foster care license. And we wanted to foster girls. The twins were the first names to come up."

"Where did you take your parenting classes?"

"Okay," Sheila said. "This is going to sound weird. Sign here first."

Sheila gestured towards the I-9. I signed and slid it back across the desk.

"Weird?"

"Well, it was a Catholic agency that approved us."

"No way. The Catholics let dykes foster kids?" My heart gave a butterfly flutter and glide.

Sheila chuckled.

"It was a little hard to wrap our minds around. Refugee Foster Care is a federal program, so they need local partners on the ground to provide services."

"So, you think I could get approved to foster? On my own? I'm single—again—and don't have a great track record in the relationship department."

My eyes instinctively darted for the floor and the monarch in my heart lay on its side, legs waggling. It was hard to talk about. I didn't want Sheila to sling worn-out platitudes like dirty socks.

youareacatch! youjusthaven'tmettherightperson! itwillhappenwhenyouleastexpectit!

"Oh, yeah. They are open to single parents. And—you're good at jumping through hoops, right? You have to be, as a teacher in California," Sheila said.

I felt my chest release.

The conversation marinated for years.

* * *

After the conversation with Sheila, I kept a downloaded pdf on my desktop—a digital brochure for prospective parents interested in Refugee Foster Care (RFC). I would open the file at least once a month to re-read, scanning the infographics that included: a map of the world with the main countries of origin (mostly in the Global South) highlighted in blue, and statistics on success once youth landed in the program (91% high school graduates, with 60% enrolled in community college and 20% enrolled at a four-year institution).

I knew about radical American Catholics, like Dorothy Day and members of the Catholic Worker Movement, who lived by the ideals of mutual aid. Maybe this Catholic agency would be governed, at least in part, by a Christian variation on the Muslim concept of sadaqah, where acts of kindness and generosity—in the name of social justice—support the collective health of a community.

Baba arrived in Amrika with a moral core that considered acts of service sacred. This sadaqah extended particularly to individuals and communities who softened his landing in the United States. In Chicago, during the first few months of his stay in Amrika, Baba used the Young Men's Christian Association (YMCA) as a literal home base. It not only provided room and board, but opportunity for connection and companionship.

Once he had established himself as a city planner in Southern California, it was the reason he volunteered for his local YMCA Board of Directors. Sadaqah made Baba light up when he talked about Andre Agassi, the former world number one tennis player, whose father was an Armenian Christian from Iran. Agassi's success and visibility were a kindness to Baba's immigrant heart.

* * *

I wasn't ready to be a foster mom on November 9, 2016, when I woke up to Donald J. Trump's first presidential victory. I wasn't ready three months later, on January 27, 2017, when he instituted the Muslim Ban. My grief and rage were lodged behind my eyes. I kept seeing floaters in my field of vision, like my brain was a suicidal disco ball, the mirrored light cutting through viscera and feasting on itself.

The only thing that softened the spinning was the understanding that—unlike 9/11—this time we had allies. Non-Muslims stood in solidarity, performing sadaqah for their brethren, and very publicly used their bodies as protest. There was a days-long occupation of the San Francisco International Airport.

As I drove an hour north to a new job at a high school in Vallejo, I followed the radio dispatches. A mid-year American History hire, I spent weeks of class time asking eleventh grade students to compare this history-in-the-making with their own notions of what it meant to be American. My students were Black and Brown, many the American-born children of immigrants. We used the Malcolm X quote, "We're not Americans, we're Africans who happen to be in America. . . . We didn't land on Plymouth Rock—that rock landed on us" to reflect on who can claim access to an American birthright. How did our identity intersect with our membership in society? What did it mean to be denied access?

My students created a chorus that momentarily slowed my grief.

"This is like the Red Scare, but for Muslims."

"Muslims are American."

"The pledge of allegiance says one nation under God. Muslims are under God too."

"I'm afraid of Trump. I'm not afraid of Muslims."

Anahita, a recent immigrant from Iran, "came out" as the only Muslim student in class on an early morning in February. All students were required to complete unit-end presentations and Anahita went first. Tall with long, expressive arms, Anahita stood at the whiteboard and described her pride in the all-girls school she had attended in Iran, a school that cultivated her mind and encouraged her creativity, where the hijab was an inconvenience but not viewed as an instrument of oppression.

"I wish I was still back home," Anahita said. "But we couldn't stay."

The first period class, often barely awake on damp, fog-thickened mornings, was alert. There was no furtive glancing at a phone on a lap. Hoods came off heads, spines loosened up. They asked Anahita questions, and she responded.

"I'm grateful to be here, but I also don't know who I am here," Anahita said. "I didn't know before the Muslim Ban, and I definitely don't know now."

* * *

By August 2018, I was ready to be a foster mom: a first-time homeowner, instead of a perennial Bay Area renter. I lived in East Oakland, in a historically Black neighborhood that was also home to a multinational immigrant community. Neighborhoods that snuggled close to mine included the wealth of Vietnamese, Guatemalan and Afghan culture, to name just a few. At the Yemeni-owned grocery store four blocks from my house, I bought 2 liter bottles of doogh, 3 kinds of pita, sangak, fenugreek seeds and cardamon pods.

I accepted another teaching job closer to home. It offered a healthier work environment, and my new class load included teaching English Language Development (ELD) classes to recent immigrants.

Besides prepping for ELD, AP Language & Composition and college prep English courses, I found time to email the address listed in the RFC digital brochure. Several weeks and a couple of phone calls later—on September 24, 2018—I received a reply, an email with eleven attachments, application forms to complete: everything from a health screening by a doctor to a house plan grid that required me to sketch the layout of my 2-bedroom, 1-bath home.

On December 19, 2018, I drove south on the I-80 to San José for my first interview with the program. San José is a thriving, racially diverse city named after the patron saint of immigrants, families, and working people. Located on the southern tip of San Francisco Bay, a vast swath of life-giving water, it was the perfect place to begin what became a year-long process to get licensed as a foster parent.

The interview coincided with an auspicious celestial omen: a brilliant meteor entering the Earth's atmosphere, leaving otherworldly wind trails across the waning sky at twilight.

A few days later, I was accepted as an RFC parent-trainee, working towards my California license to provide foster care. Like the trail of that fireball, I began crisscrossing the I-80: north to south and back again, for weekend classes and workshops. I opened my home to inspection visits from the program and submitted to hours of psychological assessments, designed to gauge my emotional readiness.

As I moved through the vetting process, I was asked about my preferences. Boy or girl? Welcoming of queer, trans and gender expansive youth? Religious or secular? African, Asian or Central American? These choices were couched around compatibility; it was important that RFC youth be acknowledged as long-term members of their foster family's home. Even so, the questions about what I wanted felt problematic. For starters, all the countries were sites of Western extraction and intervention, both historically and in-the-moment, a reality that most likely contributed to the reason youth were fleeing their home countries in the first place.

I already knew that I would be championing children from Muslim majority countries. Baba's struggle to carve a space for himself in this normatively Christian nation was family lore. I hoped to provide a home that felt culturally familiar: wrapped in the comfort of language and scent, a place where children would not have to advocate for themselves to access a house of worship, appropriate food to eat, and community celebrations and holidays.

I also advocated for male and nonbinary-identified youth to be placed with me, noting my ability to connect with masculine-of-center and genderqueer kids throughout a long career as a high school teacher.

Each discrete step indicated a commitment to place my feet gingerly in the footprints Baba had left in his wake. I too would forge a chosen family in this place. It's what Baba did for years: before he met Mom, before he gained his own citizenship, and before he sponsored his family, who began to gingerly follow him to Amrika.

* * *

As I returned north to Oakland after that first interview with RFC, I had over an hour in traffic to reflect on what—if the agency deemed me fit to undergo the training—this would mean for the rest of my life. I was about to take on a paradigm rattling endeavor without a partner, without even a coffee date on the calendar. How would this process change me? What would my family look like a year from now?

If I opened my heart to this much vulnerable possibility with a child, a partner was possible. My heart had enough space.

I am ready. I can do this. Look at how beautiful and wondrous life is.

Tracking the meteor with my eyes and breathing deep into my belly, I tapped on the brakes over and over. The trail of light corkscrewed and flipped, a phosphorescent smudge in the sky.

1998 WORLD CUP: IRAN-2, UNITED STATES-1

Mahru Elahi

easy afternoon
soccer jersey floats on breeze
we speak in soft smiles

corpuscular stain
iran swaddles my chest red
pitch green bone white

complicated pride
all our eyes wet memory
humble players dance

cross twenty third street
man spits venom on pavement
"iran hates the jews"

his cap says poet
slides down forehead in blind rage
passersby don't hear

"antisemite bitch"
fling water in self defense
single use plastic

we stumble away
duck into busy shoe store
bizarre pop soundtrack

watch death through thick glass
fifth avenue absorbs him
we bleed sweet relief

WAR PAINT

Juanita Kirton

absent is the joy and celebration no more music and dancing gone is the laughter and singing—shots heard shots fired explosions of blood screams and cries of terror woman grabbed men assaulted gagged voices cycle engines roar inferno of fire violated bodies communities plundered homes looted cadavers under rumble a massacre attack with no conscious un-human/in-human unspeakable terrifying madness rape hostages taken panic jolts a nation TV images insanity is sanitized save us from the wilderness of our grief the unbearable loss broken hearts cracked souls the desert absorbs the wretchedness and stench there are no safe rooms
RADICALIZED
birthed from a pot of oppression left to boil over bitterness mushrooms swollen wounds rage a society unseen a people unheard hopes defeated tongues are slashed no RIGHTS partitioned checkpoints NO VOTE divisions isolation rationed water health care restricted oppression is lethal with retaliation and revenge politics and power demand an eye for an eye KILL them all buried in underground tunnels the IDF cobra seeks and strikes again and again
homes buildings hospitals schools everything anything that moves camouflaged in plain sight
STRIKE - STRIKE and the virus of war s p r e a d s...
ANESTHETIZED by TV clips "IMAGES MAYBE DISTURBING"

the sea is full of their blood your blood   our blood
they cry   we pray and march for **PEACE**   **PEACE**
PEACE pleas unheard
collapse like the scorched soil and where is our shared humanity? because **ALLIED** our
bullets   our missiles   our rockets   our dilemma the great paradox **ENOUGH** of
fragmented promises shattered dreams we shoulder the wounds the cancer of war survives and thrives   return the loss ones   the taken ones   the dead ones and   **WHERE ARE**
THE CHILDREN?   your children   our children they are bruised fractured disappeared
PLEASE create a **PEACE - STOP** for the children

THE ARCH

Juanita Kirton

I want to poet a rainbow where all 7 colors are emancipated blue is blessing the babies in butterfly bubbles and

sista' green acquisitions glory and gratitude inclusive indigo values our independence as orange orbits and observes who is doing what to whom red starts the revolution as I ride my motorcycle to rally the rivers our inner vision is valued by violet she is the limb we are

the vine yuck is out of yellow she fires yesterday and says "yes" to you sometimes love gets lost in all the loneliness

but remember rainbows are always in fashion going on forever...

blue green indigos orange-red violet and yellow

DELICIOUSLY DEFIANT

Juanita Kirton

I've been loved from my head to my feet been
soothed rubbed   caressed and charmed

Been loved between dense forest over raging rivers
where streams wear down the rocks loved where
seas spilled her guts

I've been loved on mountain ridges
against glaciers carving their path loved
beyond minds capacity to dream
incoherent with possibilities

Been loved into lifetimes of bliss followed
endless roads into desolate deserts got hot
sand in my crotch
cleansed with female madness   wet with passion kisses
drank my desserts and ate meatless just to please

I've been loved on two wheels and in four
traveled light years on the backs of swans
followed into wars and behind church doors

Been loved in hospital beds with wet panties
in closets and girl's bathroom stalls
I'm waiting for Captain Jane-Way to shoot me to the stars

Been loved tightly smothered cooked beyond
recognition salt and peppered ready for a taste
loved below the belt and boxed my way in and out
loved the green off the leaves then
went into hibernation came up
through a blast of winter said,
"good-bye", but didn't mean it
said, "I do" and walked away

Been loved behind city lights in mirrored
elevators broke my heart against a subway
door gave up and let go my spine against
tarred roof tops unapologetically naked on a
Brooklyn rainbow

ANEMONE

Janine Mogannam

after everything and more
        you have brought me here
the joy   never seeming real
        like sunset on Kaanapali beach
so literal   fluorescent coral and rose
        I didn't think I deserved it
your love   vivid energy
        carries me like the wind
to this beach   armful of anemone and rose
        Waimea at sunset   a landing
a home for love   a dress made of watercolors
        lilac and lavender and sage   the wind our blessing
the Pacific our witness
        poem-prayers in hand   coral and rose
two chambers of an infinite heart
        beating rhythm with the ocean   laughter bubbles
we've been here before   on another coast
        another life almost   hard to believe
we are the same beings   we were then   hard to believe
        there are still surprises   fifteen years later
that we can say   we have withstood the tides
        I never thought I deserved this
I bathed this morning   in the ocean
        uplifted &   made buoyant
as you have done   this life   coral and rose
        I promise you   always

10.29.23

Janine Mogannam

Flying home across this stolen land two days before Halloween
and all I want is to sleep, to forget, but I can't
because the bombs are exploding in my head
and the rumble of the plane's engine
is too close to the sound I imagine
of bombs dropping on a neighborhood in Gaza.

But the neighborhoods I see below me are so complete,
trees bedecked in fall leaves like something out of a catalog:
"Complacency Direct."
And the graveyard we fly over is so sedate, so neatly arranged
as if to suggest death is but a momentary repose,
a reminder of life's comforts—

No piles of bodies laying under bloody shrouds,
the half-alive sprawled atop them, too stunned
with grief to sob, too exhausted to sleep—no zombies
here—
no open graves—no stench of death—no screaming mothers
clutching the lifeless bodies of their infants—
no skeleton children—no vampires holding puppet strings—
no mourners yearning for their own death—no ghosts
of generations of waiting and praying and begging god
to return home. For a home to return to. No.

In two days, the children of these nice neighborhoods
will play at such characters for laughs and sweet things.

They only know sweet things.
They will shed their disguises and climb
into their clean and cozy beds—no dead bodies
to cuddle to, only fanciful creatures of cloth and poly filling,
their centers white as clouds of phosphorus dust.

I don't begrudge them their innocence. I wish it
upon every child of the world. It is a child's right
to be innocent, to play at scary things
and know it is just make-believe.
To believe that a world that brings such wonder
could never become the nightmare of a midnight movie.
A graveyard for children like them.

But it is all too real.
I doze against the cold windowpane and dream
of clowns with orange-tinted faces and slick hair
roasting marshmallows over the fire of a burned
gingerbread house, using olive branches as kindling,
bones crunching beneath their feet like autumn leaves
as they dance.

SUBTEXT [DEAR HEART]

Janine Mogannam

[her face: a matte-white dream. it's all over. leave things to nature. you'll be good another day. coffee is contrary: you are still tired. an exhaustion born from years of pretending. cigarette smoke makes the world seem kinder. you vibrate, write another supernova. remembering. her tongue is too kind, a vulnerable burn. you like her scattered nature, engulfing you like the waves of the Pacific. you wade into it on darker days. turn the cup now for your fortune. leave lipstick marks for memory. coffee grounds can't predict this. she's good to you. this is easy. pick up the pen. write the words you cannot speak. she, a fountain: wishes are coins. don't overthink this. try it. try it. try it.]

UNTITLED ODE TO BODY HAIR

Janine Mogannam

First sprouting under
my chubby arms at nine,
a curiosity:

Auntie told me I was
growing up, would soon be
a young woman.

Impossible, it
seemed, to become one of them:
confident, developed

creatures who wore lipstick,
sang in Arabic, drank wine and
danced under the moon,

ripped out their body
hair with sucar wa limoon
weekly without fail.

Could I ever be
so mature? You promised yes,
another secret

strangeness dividing me
from my un-hyphenated
classmates, digging the

chasm even deeper.
I wasn't even allowed
to wear tank tops or

two-piece bathing suits,
attend birthday sleepovers,
watch PG movies.

I envied my friends,
petite girls with phones in their rooms,
furry pets who slept

on their beds, parents
who didn't force them to wear
undershirts, or

constantly lecture them,
but not their brothers,
about modesty.

Blessed body hair,
testament to an Arab
girl's dichotomy.

Rejection of an
alabaster, pristine youth
I'd never embody

but would ever be
dangling just out of my grasp,
aspirational.

Blessed body hair,
you knew what adults didn't
want us to—despite

daily reminders
of everything Arab girls
must not do, the fierce

force of ancestral
inheritance will always
assert itself in

their daughters' bodies,
stubborn fur soft and lush
as a treasured pet.

A DAUGHTER'S WORTH

Janine Mogannam

how much is this daughter worth?

a handful of sour green almonds
left on the kitchen table
next to a bowl of sea salt
a few pinches of za'atar
added to khobiz fresh from the taboun
dancing under a glimmer of zeit zatoon from ancient trees

a gold nameplate necklace, three bangle bracelets, and two hoop earrings
mama says are too large for her face
but she wears anyway when visiting aunties one, two & three
eliciting casual assessment

a star rising in black silence
when she wakes in the middle of the night
forgetting where she is
a teta's forlorn tears
when she wakes in the middle of the night
forgetting where she is
because home has become a phantom
with an unfamiliar name

a cup of bittersweet coffee turned upside down, toward the heart and read like a bedouin poem

a pot of mujaddara slightly overcooked—
although she tried—
a pair of black heels worn thin on the inside
night spent dancing in clubs she'd never name,
kissing lips she'd only met in her wildest dreams
a village of eyes upon her
a village of women who know her lineage
like the palms of their callused hands,
but cannot tell you who she really is.

the aching of distanced love,
of loss before possession

an early spring's thunderstorm
when she sits in her room with her pen
and generates her own currency.

TO BE A STORYTELLER

Anna Rose Naim

To be a storyteller is to tread into depths of unknown
To look around and bear witness
To mutter the first word, to take the first stand
To garner the attention of the bystander
To live and die by the pen

The pen that is my destiny
My specialty, my empathy, my weapon against zealotry
A kiss goodbye to my deepest wants and desires
The privilege to dream replaced by urgent duty

The pen that is my obligation
A love letter to the nation
The righteous quest towards liberation
Glory to all the martyrs
That is my declaration

The pen I will not yield
Unless it should be stolen from me
Pried out of my grasp, finger after finger, limb after limb, home after home
A heap of scribbles and thoughts grained in with the dust and rubble
Tens of thousands of stories buried under the concrete,
Each and every one of them as precious as the last

I witness again and again
Day after day

I cry
I rage
I shout into the void
I do not hear back

I keep trying
I wake up and repeat
I do not lower my weapon
What they steal with two thousand pounds of fire and destruction
I steal back with the waltz of my pen

Tomorrow's sunrise isn't promised
Holding a white flag isn't promised
Reem's fourth birthday isn't promised
I do not see beyond the smoke and the darkness
But my pen sees what I don't yet see
My pen is a time machine
My pen lives in the future

In the end, my pen will define me
Your devastation will define you

BUNKER BUSTERS AND PHOENIXES

Anna Rose Naim

There's a heaviness that stills the air anytime you're
mentioned
The kind of sorrow that doesn't only run deep, it runs
in my veins
10,452 kilometers of flawed
And when I say flawed I mean:
Where did you say you were from again? What is your last
name?
What I really mean is: what god do you worship?
But when I say god I don't mean crucifix or crescent moon
I mean the colors of a party
Trauma. Guns. Men in suits sitting on mountains of gold
A green line brought forth by those who benefit from our
division, claiming our soil as their destiny
A coming of age followed by consecutive, record breaking
years of disappointment
The years pass, the economy collapses, the port explodes
And alas, they show up with their tanks
Coffee with grandma interrupted by the sound of fighter
jets and text messages asking what has become the casual:
Are you okay?
What I really mean is, are you alive?

Come what may,
My dreams still echo in the sound of Fairuz's voice
What I love can only be described in green,

With your mighty cedars and your scent of zaatar and your
acres of olive trees

In white,
With your mountain peaks and your years of calm and
your eyes that tell tales of old Phoenicia

In red,
With your cyclamens and your valiant red cross volunteers
and your martyrs

Greek Orthodox, Maronite, Druze, Sunni, Shiaa. . .
You share my blood and that means when you bleed, I bleed
Another billion dollars to the invader couldn't dream of
taking you away
Rain or shine, alive or dead, my stardust is only to be
embedded in your soil
Bunker busters plunge deep but there's a layer, a dimension
of your body that they'll never breach

After all,
I see your lights shining underneath the buzzing skies,
You're still you and they still fall short of what they need
to conquer you

They always will

ASEXUAL INTIMACIES

Nour Kamel

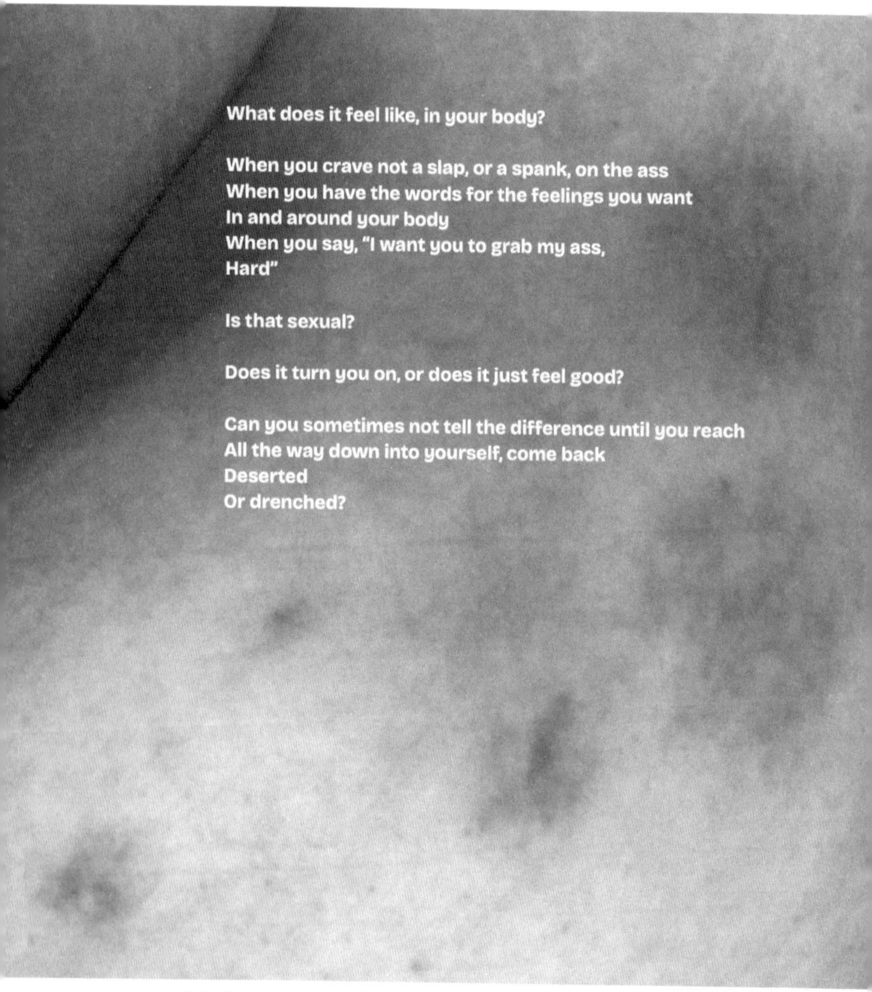

Media: Photograph

Photo Credit: Nour Kamel

ASEXUAL INTIMACIES

Nour Kamel

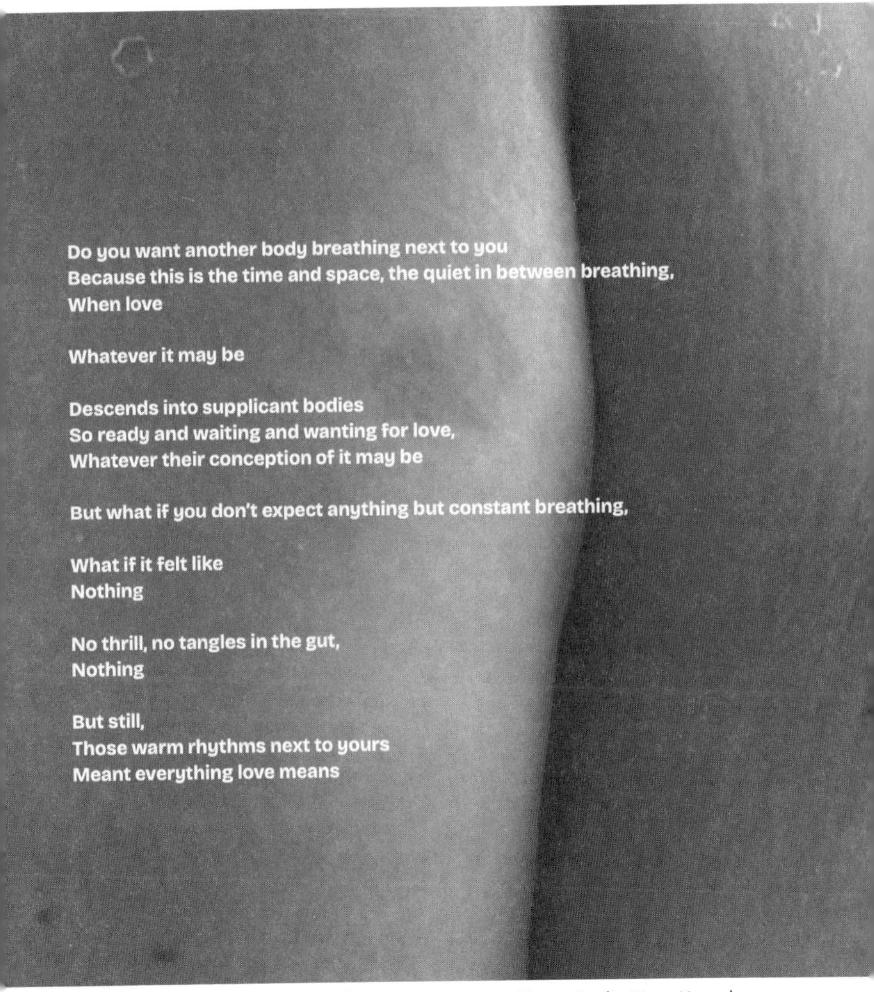

Do you want another body breathing next to you
Because this is the time and space, the quiet in between breathing,
When love

Whatever it may be

Descends into supplicant bodies
So ready and waiting and wanting for love,
Whatever their conception of it may be

But what if you don't expect anything but constant breathing,

What if it felt like
Nothing

No thrill, no tangles in the gut,
Nothing

But still,
Those warm rhythms next to yours
Meant everything love means

Media: Photograph

Photo Credit: Nour Kamel

ASEXUAL INTIMACIES

Nour Kamel

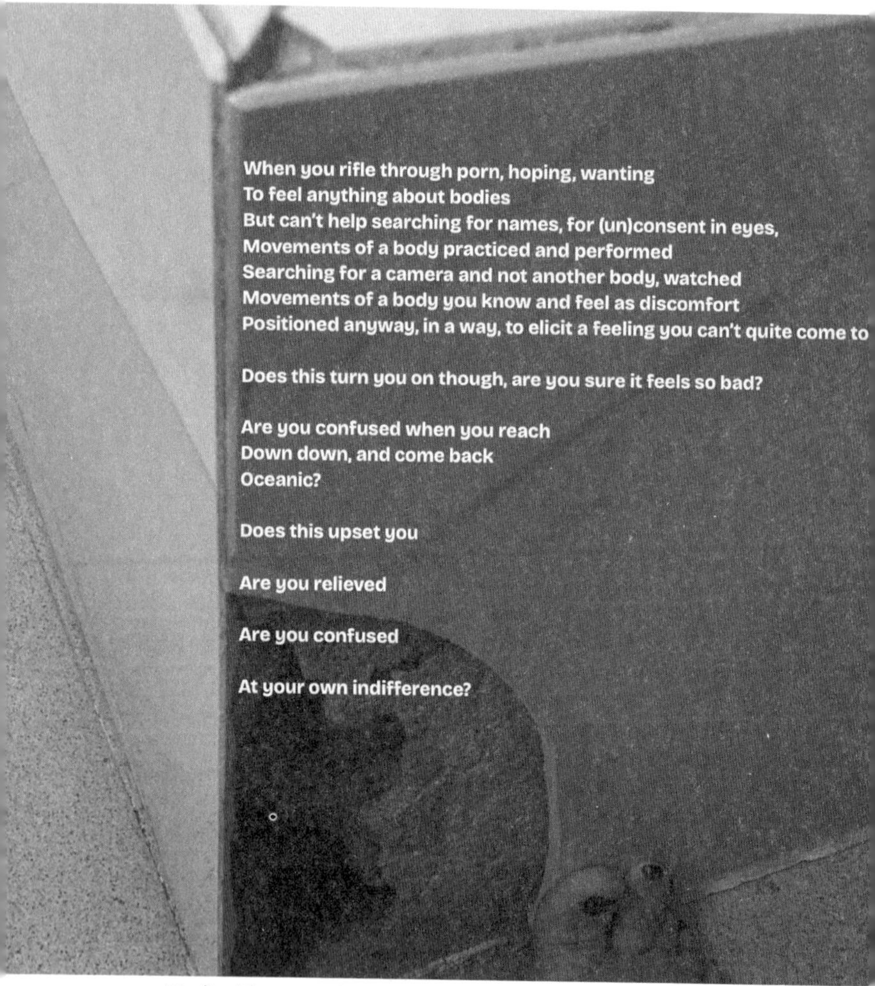

Media: Photograph

Photo Credit: Nour Kamel

ASEXUAL INTIMACIES

Nour Kamel

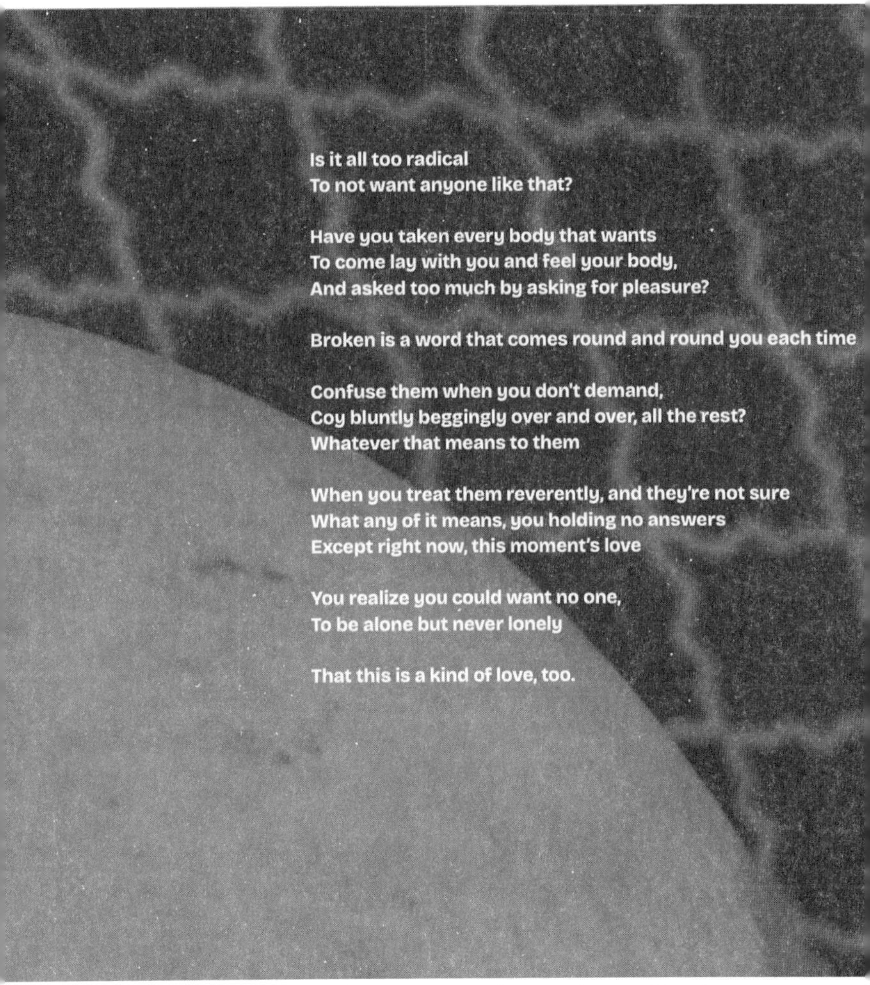

Is it all too radical
To not want anyone like that?

Have you taken every body that wants
To come lay with you and feel your body,
And asked too much by asking for pleasure?

Broken is a word that comes round and round you each time

Confuse them when you don't demand,
Coy bluntly beggingly over and over, all the rest?
Whatever that means to them

When you treat them reverently, and they're not sure
What any of it means, you holding no answers
Except right now, this moment's love

You realize you could want no one,
To be alone but never lonely

That this is a kind of love, too.

Media: Photograph Photo Credit: Nour Kamel

ASK ALICE

Nour Kamel

You gave me your anger
and took the sweetness
I thought the world was leavened on

Traded your bitterness for pastel colors
And we swapped fists for fisting
Shot glasses for tea cups
About the same small size

It couldn't contain either of us
No matter how the biscuit shrunk
Or how loud the cookie crumbs made me

Tears and flood and gushing
With rage the mome raths ate us out
How queer

The plural are many
You were all on your ones

FUCK // MAGICS

Nour Kamel

after Inua Ellams

after the houseparty / where you introduce me to the ex
you slutshamed / you drunkdrive us back to yours /
announce on the stairs to your apartment / you don't care
if i'm still on my period / you want to fuck me

i fuck with rage / i have channelled into my pussy / thinking
about you / thinking about her / sex the burgeoning hate I have
for you / in that moment / through my body / it magics into
you throwing up all that red wine / post coitus

she was so quiet / pity brewed / before ever knowing
the extent / of what you did to her / before knowing what you
could do / how i should have used every orgasm / to manifest
misery / you naked and retching over the bowl / i pat you
on the head / slip back into your bed / summon with
my clit a peaceful evening / for all your exes

B/C OUR RELATIONSHIPS TO EACH OTHER ARE DOCUMENTED – *ANDREA ABI-KARAM*

Nour Kamel

delete everything
in fact don't do anything
in hopes no one finds out enough to out you
in fact there is nothing to delete
neither of us on the dating app
mention the word date, or love, or sex,
not lesbian of course
leave no evidence
dance around the subject unsure
who the other is
where they're at in terms of out
but not out out
have you done this before? no one has done this before
it is new and terrifying each time

not the terror tinged with excitement of new love
the terror of will you out me to my family
will you blackmail me
will you make me love you
feel vulnerable
and will you take all that to hurt me emotionally
make me suffer
abandonment and shame suffer
honor killing suffer

lose everyone and everything I've built suffer
have nothing in our society suffer

will you make love to me, finally, on a bed of cameras
document and save each photo and word I send you
for the courts of debauchery and hate and crime,
or to jerk off to?
another example of an untrue body, not right
for loving the wrong type

will we break each others hearts into pieces because
we just can't be
anything more than what we are, in the dark, in stairwells
fingers only ever worm under clothes
never ripped or lovingly taken off
what would our mothers say?
what would the fathers do?

يسقط يسقط حكم العائلة[1]

1 down, down with family rule

IN THE SUNROOM, WHERE YOU KEEP A SPARE BED

Nour Kamel

Desperately, like it's always the last time
hungry, because sometimes it is
for the longest time, and I don't love you.

I love the smell of the air where you live,
elevated, beachy, sea salt cut, coming
fall we both love. We are not in love,
sex on each others' bodies. we don't ache

in the dark alone, don't think about each other,
unroll our warmth, don't text for weeks til we do.
All fleshy as you tumble me around
a single bed, I all tits and spit know

where to touch, you sweating on me
a pillow princess oh both making sounds
of what we think the other needs to get

through whatever the fuck we're doing here

FEMME WILDS

Nour Kamel

you belong to everyone so look it too clamped in gold hoops chemical relaxer hair khishin[1] rites of eurocentric womanhood passed colonizer-to-media-to-mother-to-daughter not a long term solution? cut it off ya wad ya bit[2] for a couple of miles, anyway, til the tits come in near the onset of pubescent peak hair everywhere pull the honey from the comb sweet sweet squeeze of howling lemon cure thick dark troubles in that itchy sweater between legs blood cupped matted a natural repellant/aphrodisiac shove in some white gold keep going keep some body leave stretchmarks to grow behind forests no one should ever see how the body shifts those violet faultline fissures cracking to withstand the all of you everything you could devour in a handsome handmade dress that fit just you

just you

it'll be more useful as a tent worn to just the slit of eyes otherwise sun will darken you undesirable under there, under wear, tear the neon orange lipstick a beacon of sentience it'll attract the wrong crowd of wolves who'll tear your mouth to silence tho a good lesson for learning to hide deserted for hiding a lifetime for hiding in reflective

---

1 خشن
2 يا واد يا بت

surfaces too no one wants to see you not an object, not not an object touched by time and tired stay wary cool uncaring, narcissa didn't drown the myth of her doesn't exist on pondfish lips and you'd never be allowed to be narcissus not here no, your knees would grow mossy with too little use and you! you have too much labor still to do, not for yourself but for those nautical onlookers, hide the wildflowers for feelers hidden in hair to help forget you haven't it in you to survive this trek in a body like yours

a body like yours

unchosen, then chosen again and again and again, only yours when they're not looking when the only hair you're allowed to grow grows back so long you tie it around your neck the boys will tug it for shelter propriety arousal so watch out for the plush violence splayed beneath your feet, behind your bottom the girls grow like mushrooms too pretending to love you only in certain light, flavors, swallow enough then perhaps you can burrow into sky into where stars live waiting for a mouth that looks like it kissed celestials once, magic maybe will help guide you some when it all burns out when everything else is done selling you to you for their own safety, good, you really will need shelter tho you'll have to fashion it yourself from borrowed parts some hyperjointed bones to stretch painfully, a hollow horn to summon no one, a packet of chiclets to keep things bubble fresh, a menstrual cup that runneth over with your blood only
your blood always.

FASTING

Najlaa Manout

Want and need
Go hand in hand
She sustained
From water and
Bread
Her hunger
Her thirst
Will cleanse her
From the curse they casted on her
Their memory would fade away
Her lust will wither In
the absence of food
She will grow stronger
Against her want for them
Days Passed
Weight lost
Exhaustion ruled her days
Her lips dry Her eyes half-open
Neither fast was broken
Nor their spell

INFORMATION IS ALIVE

KT Abadir-Mullally

The digital age is a beautiful and devastating time to be alive. As a digital archivist, I am inspired and haunted by the lack of sustainable digital preservation practices. Our digital files that store our communication, memories, and labor are rotting all around us. Our digital media carriers are becoming damaged and our files are corrupting due to bitrot and data decay. Keeping our digital mark accessible relies on the cloud storage facilitated by private corporations with server sites that are destroying our access to clean water. On top of the environmental consequences, long term storage solutions require a sustained influx of money. Our digital files are hosted on proprietary software with corporations such as Google, Microsoft, and Amazon, who are invested in arms manufacturing. There is no guarantee we will be able to open our files when we no longer have access to the host software once a company goes under. I pray these companies will go under. Archivists have work arounds to software becoming inaccessible, such as virtual machines, and perhaps those will be more common one day. Our sustainability and preservation efforts cannot keep up with our cultural production.

Western ideas of preservation are linked to ownership and prestige because western ideas of power rely on ownership. Archivists are fighting light, humidity, pests, temperature, chemical reactions, and preparing for natural disasters to maintain institutional ownership over information. Ideally, we are also fighting for sustained public access. In 2025, we are chipping away at the barriers to access of our ivory towers but the legacy remains.

What if we are more comfortable with information disappearing? Or taking different forms? What if we let information die and we become comfortable with being forgotten or only remembered as a sliver of ourselves? With climate change actively destroying life as we know it, trust in information keeps me going. Information will live on in a different way outside of all the preservation efforts by people like me.

I believe in information magic. When I say information, I mean anything and everything. Information is what is conveyed or represented by a particular arrangement or sequence of things. Imagine everything that is coming at you at all times from all directions. We are very good at picking, observing and receiving an abundance of information then extracting what we need from it in the moment we receive it. Information is all around us. In everyone. In everything. When I visualize the concept of information, I see a gooey sticky capricious thing that is loudly ungovernable. The idea of information reminds me a lot of queerness in the way that it ignores borders and finds new ways to move through communities and people.

Acknowledging the agency of ideas fights off my premature feelings of loss. So much of my love for the people around me lives in these digital forms that will not be accessible in the future.

Ideas survive in different forms and access to the past is not linear. I am supposedly a descendant from a culture that is rich in rituals around life and death, see: the pyramids. The international fascination with Egypt, specifically a 3000-year period that began over 5000 years ago, was globalized in the 19th century due to western greed. The empire of Ancient Egypt was eradicated by Roman and Greek conquest and traditions of Northeast Africans were destroyed. The spiritual traditions are continuously disrespected today. Objects and, more importantly, bodies were buried with elaborate strategies. The bodies, meant to be left alone, to sink into the earth, and decay, have been excavated for a variety of purposes from public scholarship to medical cannibalism. Financial gain is the driving force of this brand of grave robbing. Egyptian and Sudanese bodies and objects travel internationally while there are visa limitations and travel bans preventing Egyptian and Sudanese people from entering the countries where their ancestors' bodies are, further disenfranchising descendants. Protecting the past is respecting the choices individuals make while they are alive. In academia and in colonialism, there is an assumption that current scholars, anthropologists, archeologists, or archivists know better than the individuals who created the very objects they want to restore and keep safe.

Motifs of Northeast African culture from 3200 BC--30 BCE survive on a global scale in the 21st century. Symbols and motifs are restructured for horror films, ankh tattoos, the Washington Monument, pornography, carnival rides, jewelry, and scholarship centers in Philadelphia. In the United States symbols of Ancient Egypt succeed in making money because they have been detached from spiritual practice and blood lines to attach to empire and power.

The legacy of violence in the extraction of North African histories is interrogated in Afrofuturist artwork by African diasporic artists and Egyptian artists such as Kara Walker, Lauren Halsey, Ghada Amer, Maren Hassinger, and Mahmoud Mokhtar. Afrofuturist artwork utilizing motifs of Ancient Egypt and Ancient Nubia challenge the misinformation of European ownership. Tension between contemporary Egyptian communities and the African diaspora is based in anti-blackness within Egyptian culture. Artists reclaim symbols of Ancient Egypt to fight against oppression and colonial invaders by remembering empires before colonization. Contemporary artworks return icons to their spiritual contexts rather than utilizing the symbols as tools for political power. In Iman Issa's artist statement in Flight into Egypt, she calls Ancient Egypt a concept or essence that awakens at different times. No matter how dormant, the essence is waiting for the right time to come forward and be re-remembered. This is Information Magic.

As a baby dyke, I was desperately looking for my queer Egyptian representation. I've always had Umm Kulthum, but I was searching for explicit queerness and joy. I searched in archives but found that narratives focused on the trauma gay SWANA men experience in their home countries. I could barely find examples of SWANA LGBTQ+ history regarding women or transgender people. I was living in Los Angeles, spending a significant amount of time at the ONE Archives, the largest repository of LGBTQ+ materials in the world. At the ONE Archives, the materials in the Egypt subject file were several articles on the Cairo 52. On May 11, 2001, fifty-two men were violently arrested on the Queen Boat, a floating gay nightclub on the Nile. I was angry, I am still angry, about the reality of homophobia and violence. I was angry that the largest repository of LGBTQ+ materials in the world contained a mere sliver of the queer SWANA experience—and that its narrative of Egyptian queerness was exclusively in the stories of police brutality and shame. The omission of records supports the narrative that white saviors need to save brown queer people, and that the only queer people in the SWANA region are gay men. The lack of a full story is used to justify US imperialism of the SWANA region and the villainization of the Arab world. In reaction to that I created a collecting project committed to documenting, preserving, and sharing access to celebration, stories, and moments of joy by diasporic, queer SWANA artists and creators. The collecting project is sleeping as we are navigating the surveillance state.

In the last decade there has been an explosion of SWANA queer organizing in art collectives, dance parties, grant programs, community meet-ups, activist groups, and mutual aid networks. The death of Sarah Hegazi radicalized queer Egyptian and queer SWANA community. In 2025, we are loud as queer SWANA people and as SWANA dykes. We are also hyper-surveilled because we say no to pinkwashing and "fuck Israeli propaganda" and we stand against occupation and apartheid.

Information is a threat. Information is a tool of liberation. Israel understands the crucial power of information in self-determination. According to the Preliminary Report from Librarians and Archivists with Palestine: Israeli Damage to Archives, Libraries, and Museums in Gaza, October

2023–January 2024, Israel damaged or completely demolished the following 22 archives, museums, and libraries: Central Archives of Gaza City, Gaza City Hall (Gaza City), Gaza Municipal Library (Gaza City), Omari Mosque and Library (Gaza City), Al-Nahda Library, Diana Tamari Sabbagh Library in the Rashad al-Shawa Cultural Center (Al-Rimal, Gaza City), Lubbud Library, Kana'an Educational Development Institute (Al-Rimal, Gaza City), Enaim Library, Samir Mansour Bookshop and Library (Gaza City), Al-Shorouq Al-Daem Library, Islamic University of Gaza Library (Gaza City), Al-Israa University Library and National Museum (near Gaza City), Al-Quds Open University Library (Gaza City), Jawaharlal Nehru Library, Al-Azhar University (Gaza City), Akkad Museum, Cultural Kararah Museum, Deir Al-Balah Museum, Ibrahim Abu Sha'ar Heritage Diwan (Southeast of Rafah), Khudari Museum, Al-Qarara Cultural Museum, also known as the Khan Younis Museum (Khan Younis), Rafah Museum (Rafah), and Shahwan Museum. I name each precious space of information sharing because each site had boundless capacity to inspire, educate, and revolutionize.

There is not a world in which the violence in Sudan, Palestine, Haiti, Congo, Yemen, Lebanon, Kashmir, Hawaii, or Iran will ever be justified. Regardless of how hard imperialism tries to erase and destroy a people, we will never be forgotten. Our strategies of survival, regardless if they are saved on the cloud or published in a book, will come back to us when we need it. As a digital archivist and an angry dyke, I will leave you with the knowledge that digital media is not forever and international organizing and relationships will tear down borders.

RESOURCE LIST

note: all @usernames refer to Instagram.

Migrant Domestic Workers

- Egna Legna Besidet Collective @egnalegna / egnalegna.org
- Migrant Workers' Action @migrantworkersaction / mwaction.org
- This is Lebanon @thisislebanon961 / thisislebanon.site

Sudan

- Hope and Haven Refugees Organization @hopeand-havenrefugees / hopeandhavenforrefugees.org
- Khartoum Aid Kitchen @khartoum_aid_kitchen / khartoumaidkitchen.org
- Mutual Aid Sudan Coalition @mutual.aid.sudan / mutualaidsudan.org
- Nas Al Sudan @nasalsudan

Congo

- Focus Congo @focuscongo / focuscongo.com
- Panzi Foundation @panzifoundation / panzifoundation.org
- Friends of the Congo @congofriends / friendsofthecongo.org
- Team Congo @teamcongo.rdc / teamcongordc.com

Tigray

- Omna Tigray @omnatigray / omnatigray.com
- Tigray Action Committee @tigrayact / tigrayactioncommittee.com
- Tigray Disaster Relief Fund / tdrfund.org
- Tigray Art Collective @tigrayartcollective

Armenia

- All for Armenia @all_for_armenia
- Galas LGBTQ+ Armenian Society @galasorg / galasla.org
- Mother Armenia @motherarmenia_bayarea
- Women's Resource Center of Armenia @wrc_armenia / womenofarmenia.org

Hawai'i

- Kanaeokana @kanaeokana / kanaeokana.org
- 'Āina Momona @ainamomona/ kaainamomona.org
- Kānaka Autonomy @kanakautonomy
- O'ahu Water Protectors @oahuwaterprotectors / oahuwaterprotectors.org
- Protect Mauna a Wākea @protectmaunakea / mkea.info

Indigenous Sovereignty and Activism

- The Red Nation @therednationmovement / therednation.org
- Giniw Collective @giniwcollective / giniw.org
- Lakota People's Law Project @lakotalaw / lakotalaw.org
- Urban Indian Health Institute @urbanindianhealthinstitute / uihi.org

Migrant Rights

- National Day Laborer Organizing Network @daylaborernetwork / ndlon.org
- Pilsen Alliance @pilsenalliance / thepilsenalliance.org
- Al Otro Lado @alotrolado_org / alotrolado.org

Afghanistan

- Uplift Afghanistan Fund @upliftafgfund / upliftafghanistan.org
- Afghan Cultural Society @afghanculturalsociety / afghanculturalsociety.org
- ALO: Afghan LGBTQ Organization @afghanlgbt / iglyo.org/members/alo
- Aftaab Magazine @aftaabmagazine / aftaabmag.com

Palestine

- Amal for Palestine @amal_for_palestine / amal4palestine.org
- Connecting Humanity @connectgaza / connecting-humanity.org
- Gaza Funds @gaza.funds / gazafunds.com
- alQaws @alqaws_org / alqaws.org

Lebanon

- Helem: @helemlebanon / helem.net
- Queer Mutual Aid Lebanon: patreon.com/qmalebanon
- Haven for Artists: @havenforartists / havenforartists.org
- The A Project: @mashroualef / theaproject.org

Iran

- Collective for Black Iranians @collectiveforblackiranians / collectiveforblackiranians.org
- From Iran @from____iran

Syria

- Syria Untold @syriauntold / syriauntold.com

Yemen

- Yemeni Women Archive @yemeniwomenarchive / ywarchive.org

Iraq

- IraQueer @iraqueer_organization / iraqueer.org

Egypt

- Rainbow Egypt @rainbowegyptorg_ / rainbowegypt.org

Queer Religious and Cultural Organizations

- Coptic Queer Stories @copticqueerstories
- Halal and Queer Collective @halalandqueer / haqcollective.org
- Muslims for Progressive Values @mpvusa / mpvusa.org
- The Muslim Alliance for Sexual and Gender Diversity @themasgd / masgd.org

CONTRIBUTORS

Amal Ishaque is a Jeddah born, Pakistani femme poet based in unceded Musqueam, Squamish and Tsleil-Waututh territories (Vancouver, BC). Their writing has been published in various literary journals and anthologies including *Queer and Muslim: On Faith, Family and Healing, The World that Belongs to Us: An Anthology of Queer Poetry from South Asia, Writing the Walls Down: A Convergence of LGBTQ Voices, Pulsamos: LGBTQ Poets Respond to the Pulse Nightclub Shooting, Glass Poetry Journal* and more. Their art practice moves across disciplines, visioning liberatory collective futures. Amal has been organizing at the intersecting frontlines of Palestine solidarity and anti-pinkwashing resistance for many years, along with involvement in multiple other movements. Website: rosewaterpoet.com / Instagram @amal_ishaque

As a first-generation Chaldean Iraqi who grew up in Ontario, Canada, **Amir Patros** investigates themes related to multigenerational resilience and the disconnect between body and home in relation to nomadism. This has resulted in the manifestation of Prince Zorah, a fantastical alter-ego prominently featured in Amir's work. His journey involves realistic and mythological imagery to analogize real feelings within marginalization and deep-rooted care. The introspection and admiration of texts and media such as Take care of Yourself by Sundus Abdul Hadi and The Little Prince by Antoine de Saint-Exupéry has influenced Amir's love of creating folktales based on resistance. (IG: @princezorah)

Andrea Abi-Karam is a trans, SWANA, punk poet-performer cyborg. They are the author of *EXTRATRANSMISSION* (Kelsey Street Press, 2019), *Villainy* (Nightboat Books, Sept 2021), and with Kay Gabriel, they co-edited *We Want It All: An Anthology of Radical Trans Poetics* (Nightboat Books, 2020). They are currently writing a poet's novel about crushes & a murder mystery.

Anna Rose Naim (Arabic: آنا روز نعيم) was born in 1999 to Lebanese parents and grew up between West Virginia, Pennsylvania, and Lebanon. In recent years, she has taught English in Madrid and pursued an MFA in Creative Writing at Wilkes University. She is a fiction writer interested in a wide array of genres, her pride in her Levantine culture always serving as the vanguard of her work. You can view more of her work at @annarosenaim on Instagram.

Arielle Zaytoun Sonnenschein is a poet/playwright, songwriter, actor and event professional. Her work explores intersections of Arab American and Ashkenazi identity, queerness, grief, diaspora and feminine rage. She completed her training at the Stella Adler Studio in New York with a focus on classical theatre. Her band Feral Future (active from 2012-2016 Western Medical Records) examined themes of feminism and queerness. In 2018 she curated Treasures of the Night in collaboration with This Is Austin Not That Great. She currently works at the Weisman Art Museum as Event Manager, is an ensemble member of the Commutator Collective and collective member of The World To Come Twin Cities. She lives in Minneapolis, MN on Dakota land with her spouse.

Christina Hajjar is a Lebanese artist, writer, and cultural worker based in Winnipeg on Treaty 1 Territory. Her practice considers intergenerational inheritance, domesticity, and place through diaspora, body archives, and cultural iconography. As a queer femme and first-generation subject, she is invested in the poetics of process, translation, and collaborative labour. Hajjar was a recipient of the 2020 PLATFORM Photography Award and she received an honourable mention for the 2021 Emerging Digital Artists Award. She is passionate about independent publishing and edits *Herizons Magazine* (on feminism), *Carnation Zine* (on diaspora and displacement) and *qumra journal* (on world cinema). Her zine *Diaspora Daughter / Diaspora Dyke* won Artzine of the Year in 2021. Learn more at christinahajjar.com.

Diya Abbas is a first-generation Pakistani Butch from the Midwest. Her poems and essays can be found in *Sinister Wisdom, Adroit, North American Review, Michigan Quarterly* and others. She believes the poem is a clock. The poem makes time. Find more of her muses at diyabbas.com

Elias Bouderdaben is an Amazigh Muslim genderfuck living on occupied and unceded Piscataway and Nacotchtank land, who firmly believes art cannot exist outside of activism. Their artistic mediums include poetry and printmaking. They explore concepts of gender, sexuality, pleasure, and diaspora at the intersections of race and spirituality in these mediums.

Eva Roslin (they/she) is a queer, disabled, non-binary writer and poet from Canada who writes dark fantasy and horror.

Their family origins are rooted in Isfahan and Vanadzor. Their works have appeared in publications that include *Pretend You Don't See Her* (Kandisha Press) and others. By day, they work as a curator of books.

Hanan Tuffaha is an MFA student in poetry at Umass Boston, currently residing in Saugus, MA. She writes poetry about identity, specifically relating to her queerness and Palestinian identities, as well as trauma and mental health.

Janine Mogannam is a diasporic Palestinian poet, librarian, and literary curator born and raised in San Francisco (unceded Ramaytush Ohlone land). Her work uplifts and celebrates the intersections of queer, Palestinian, feminist and San Franciscan legacies, bringing our experiences to light and fighting for the beautiful and liberated futures we deserve. Janine is a member of the Radius of Arab American Writers and Still Here San Francisco and is an alum of the VONA and Interdisciplinary Writers' Lab workshops. As a Creating Queer Community fellow with the National Queer Arts Festival, Janine curated the festival's first queer and trans Arab American performance. Janine's writing can be found in *The Margins, Apogee, The Quarry,* the anthologies *Ask the Night for a Dream: An Anthology of Palestinian Writing from the Diaspora* and *Heaven Looks Like Us: Palestinian Poetry,* and elsewhere.

Juanita Kirton is a Black, gay, African American, elder women. She earned an MFA from Goddard College. She is the 2024 1st place winner *of Oprelle Publication/Matter Anthology.* Juanita is recently published in *AVOW (Ameri-*

can Veterans Women Magazine), Mom Egg Review, Narrative, Persimmon Tree, Stillwater Review, Stone Canoe, Veterans Voices. She is a member of Women Who Write, IWWG and Women Reading Aloud workshops; a teaching artist at Crossing Point Arts and a Trauma informed facilitator for Warrior Writers. She conducts writing workshops at Kirkridge Retreat Center. Her chapbook, *Letters to My Father,* published (2020). Juanita is working on her first a full-length book of poetry. Riding her motorcycle keeps her sane.

Khadija Pitts-Ceesay (she/her) is an African-American, Lebanese and queer poet from Pittsburg, Kansas. She has been writing poetry since 2014 about her sexuality, religion and race in order to understand herself better and owes much of the ideas behind her work to her relationships with family, both good and bad. She received both her B.A. and M.A. from Pittsburg State University where she studied English literature and poetics. During her free time, she enjoys reading, crocheting, and spending time at home with her wife and two cats.

KT Abadir-Mullally is a Coptic Irish American installation and social practice artist based in Philadelphia. As an artist and archivist who works in digital preservation, they are curious about the movement of information and how much or little control we have over what is remembered or forgotten. Through sculpture and relationship building, their work debates the fragileness of our modern cultural production and the desire for ideas and information to die. Their research dives into fear, hybridity, queerness, collective thinking, grief, and cultural loss. Abadir-Mullally's work has been included in exhibitions in Philadelphia, New York, and Los Angeles. Their work has been funded by the Leeway Art and Change Grant and the Bartol Foundation. Abadir-Mullally's artwork has been published in *Queer Rain: Belonging, Dardishi Issue 2: Healing, and Coptic Queer Stories.* Abadir-Mullally is a member of Batikh Batikh, an artist collective, pop-up cinema and gallery centering SWANA women, queer and local artists in Philadelphia. Above all else, they are passionate about diasporic queer Southwest Asian and North African joy and complexity, and the agency of the living to decide how their narratives are preserved.

Lamya H (she/they) is a queer Muslim writer and organizer living in New York City. Their memoir *HIJAB BUTCH BLUES* (February, 2023 from Dial Press/Penguin Randomhouse) won the Brooklyn Public Library Book Prize and a Stonewall Non-fiction Book Award, and was a finalist for Lambda Literary and Publishing Triangle Awards. Lamya's work has appeared in *Los Angeles Review of Books, Salon, Autostraddle, Vice,* and others. She has received fellowships from Lambda Literary and Queer|Arts. Lamya's organizing work centers around creating spaces for LGBTQ+ Muslims, fighting Islamophobia, Palestine and prison abolition. In her free time, she eats lots of desserts baked by her partner, plays board games with whoever she can corral, and works on her goal of traveling to every subway stop in the city. She has never run a marathon. Find her on Twitter and IG: @lamyaisangry

Mahru Elahi (they/them/او) is a queer Iranian American femme. They have received support from Lambda Literary,

Tin House, Hedgebrook, VONA, Antioch University Los Angeles, and UCLA Extension Writers' Program. Their poetry and prose is published in *Seventh Wave*, *Black Warrior Review*, *Foglifter*, *Multiplicity* and *Fireweed*, among others. Mahru urges you to act against genocide and towards a love that cannot be acknowledged by empire.

Melina McConatha is a multispecies mutual aid scholar, abolitionist, and queer ecologist that lives on land once cared for by the Lenni-Lenape people. Her work is informed by roots in the Deep South and Iranian diaspora.

Micaela Kaibni Raen is a Palestinian American creator, cultural worker, lesbian mother, femme-dyke, and global Queer/Trans rights activist. She grew up in the Little Arabia community in California and graduated from Chapman University. During that time, she participated in the Radius of Arab American Writers, Inc., N.O.W., ACT UP!, and Queer Nation. She is most known for *QueerTatreez*, a style of visual art and poetics inspired by Indigenous Palestinian Tatreez embroidery. She received a Yalda Award for Poetry as well as nominations for The Pushcart Prize and Best of the Net. Her work appears in *Bint el Nas; Mizna; Qafiyah Review; The Poetry of Arab Women; Yellow Medicine Review; El Ghourabaa; Ask the Night for a Dream; and Heaven Looks Like Us.* Web Site: micaelakaibniraen.blogspot.com / Instagram: @micaelakaibniraen / Linktree: linktr.ee/micaelakaibniraen

Miqlae is a trans Palestinian Dyke based in Minneapolis. Other poetry can be found in P.Y.M. 's Ghassan Kanafani arts scholarship 2022 and at @d2wo4 (Dykes 2 Watch out 4 MSP). All work is inspired by and dedicated to the courage of Gaza and Queer love globally.

Najlaa Manout is a genderqueer queer writer, and a PhD student in Media and Culture Studies from Morocco, living in Germany for the past seven years. Their work explores sex, absurdity, desire and darkness. Growing up in Casablanca, a big city where they felt small, and navigating their twenties in Europe through dysphoria, shaped their writing. They use they/them and he/him pronouns and invite readers to sit at a dirty table and find beauty in the mess.

Nikki Luna is a Lebanese-American genderqueer poet, visual artist, make-up artist, and archival researcher based in Mnisóta Makhóčhe (Minnesota) on the occupied ancestral and contemporary homeland of the Dakota and Anishinaabe peoples. Nikki's work with poetry and archives has included organizing the Mizna Arab Arts' Writing Collective, teaching writing workshops with Querencia Press, serving as a judge for the Minnesota Book Award, performing public poetry readings with Mizna Arab Arts and No Borders @ Minneapolis People's Pride, and researching with the archives at the Newberry Library in Chicago, IL and the Don Kelly Research Collection of Gay Literature and Culture in College Station, TX. When they were little, Nikki dreamed of writing books, creating art, and being a queer mermaid. She honors those desires through literary community building, genre-fluid artistic practices, and growing amongst chosen family. IG: @nikki__luna

Noor Al-Dayeh Noor Al-Dayeh (they/them) is a Syrian-Palestinian artist and author from Los Angeles, CA. The queer child of Southwest Asian and North African (SWANA) immigrants (a Syrian father and Jordanian-Palestinian mother) much of Al-Dayeh's work critiques the orientalist gaze as it pertains to intersectional identities within the SWANA region. A Highest Honors graduate of Emory University, their senior thesis & post-undergraduate work documents the lives of queer SWANA women and gender non-conforming individuals and their safe spaces, in their ethnography, *Hayati: My Life / My Love*. Having volunteered at the Lesbian Herstory Archives in NYC and currently at the June L. Mazer Lesbian archives, they are dedicated to the preservation and protection of queer & BIPOC communities and histories. Al-Dayeh also specializes in various types of digital and film photography, writing practices, research, public speaking, on-set production positions, and social media advocacy. Visit Noor's Website for more: noor.aldayeh.com and follow them on every platform: @ nooraldayeh / Photography Instagram Acct: @capturethenoor

Nour Kamel is a writer, editor, and baker from Egypt working through the poetics of food, family, community, oppression, language, queerness & gender. They believe in a free Palestine. Her chapbook *Noon* is part of the New-Generation African Poets series, and they organize experimental collaborations, writing & research with Kusbarra Collective.

Sarah E. Azizi's previous publications include *Rattle, Fahmidan, Wrongdoing, The Coop, Emerge Literary Journal,*

Free State Review, Bell Press & *Querencia Press.* Her debut Collection, *Make a Wish*, was published by ELJ editions in 2025. She lives with her daughter, among friends, family of choice, and piles of unfinished work. Follow her all over: @SEAziziWrites

WIDAD is a queer Palestinian Christian physician, public health practitioner, and poet.

OTHER BOOKS FROM *SINISTER WISDOM*

SWANA Dykes, edited by Khadijah Pitts-Ceesay and Nikki Luna, 2026

The Complete Works of Pat Parker (10th Anniversary Edition), edited by Julie R. Enszer, 2026

The Dyke and the Dybbuk, Ellen Galford, 2026

Acts of Resistance, Cheryl Clarke, 2026

Essential Poems by Pat Parker, edited by SaraEllen Strongman, 2025

Black Lesbian in White America and Other Writings, Anita Cornwell, edited by Briona Simone Jones, 2025

Melting in Your Mouth: The Early Work of Chocolate Waters, Chocolate Waters, 2025

S/HE, Minne Bruce Pratt, 2024

Blue Heat: A Portfolio of Poems and Drawings, Alexis De Veaux, 2024

Hungerheart: The Story of a Soul, C. Marshall St. John, 2025

The Pagoda: A Lesbian Community By the Sea, Rose Norman, 2024

The Highest Apple: Sappho and the Lesbian Poetic Tradition, Judy Grahn, 2023

Fire-Rimmed Eden: Selected Poems, Lynn Lonidier, 2023

A Sturdy Yes of a People: Selected Writings, Joan Nestle, 2022

Para las Duras: Una Fenomonologia Lesbiana / For the Hard Ones: A Lesbian Phenomenology, tatiana de la tierra, 2018

Sister Love: The Letters of Audre Lorde and Pat Parker 1974-1989, edited by Julie R. Enszer, 2018

What Can I Ask: New and Selected Poems 1975-2014, Elana Dykewomon, 2015

Living as a Lesbian, Cheryl Clarke, 2014

Crime Against Nature, Minne Bruce Pratt, 2013

Sinister Wisdom is a multicultural lesbian literary & art journal founded in 1976. *Sinister Wisdom* works to create multi-class, multicultural, multi-gender, multi-racial, world-wide intergenerational queer and lesbian spaces. Through publishing quarterly issues, a Sapphic Classics book series, and offering educational programs, Sinister Wisdom nurtures lesbian communities. *Sinister Wisdom* is a living archive that celebrates the multiplicity of lesbian identities across races, classes, genders, abilities, and lived experiences. *Sinister Wisdom* recognizes the power of language and art to create radical, empowering, resilient, and joyous sanctuaries that build and sustain vibrant lesbian futures.

Former editors and publishers:

Harriet Ellenberger (aka Desmoines)
and Catherine Nicholson (1976-1981)
Michelle Cliff and Adrienne Rich (1981-1983)
Michaele Uccella (1983-1984)
Melanie Kaye/Kantrowitz (1983-1987)
Elana Dykewomon (1987-1994)
Caryatis Cardea (1991-1994)
Akiba Onada-Sikwoia (1995-1997)
Margo Mercedes Rivera-Weiss (1997-2000)
Fran Day (2004-2010)
Julie R. Enszer & Merry Gangemi (2010-2013)
Julie R. Enszer (2013-)

Sinister Wisdom is a US non-profit organization; donations to support the work and distribution of *Sinister Wisdom* are welcome and appreciated, including legacy gifts in wills and trusts.